Wild Bees

Also by Martin Harrison:

Poetry
1975
Truce
The Distribution of Voice
The Kangaroo Farm
Summer
Music

Essays
Who Wants to Create Australia?

Martin Harrison

Wild Bees
New and Selected Poems

Shearsman Books
Exeter

Published in the United Kingdom in 2008 by
Shearsman Books Ltd
58 Velwell Road   Published simultaneously in Australia by the
Exeter EX4 4LD   University of Western Australia Press, Perth, WA.

ISBN 978-1-84861-008-8

Copyright © Martin Harrison, 1993, 1997, 2001, 2005, 2008.

The right of Martin Harrison to be identified as the author of this work has been asserted by him in accordance with the Copyrights, Designs and Patents Act of 1988. All rights reserved.

Acknowledgements
Many of these poems have appeared previously in my collections *The Distribution of Voice* (University of Queensland Press), *The Kangaroo Farm* (Paper Bark Press), *Summer* (Paper Bark Press) and from two limited-edition books, *Music: Prose and Poems* (Vagabond Press) and *Truce* (Hawk Press). I am very grateful to the publishers of these collections.

Poems in this volume have appeared in *Antipodes*, *Age Monthly Review*, *Aspect*, *Chautauqua Literary Journal*, *Heat*, *Island*, *London Review of Books*, *Manoa* (Hawai'i), *Meanjin*, *Overland*, *Poetry* (Chicago), *Poetry International* (San Diego), *Poetry International* (http://international.poetryinternationalweb.org), *Poets on Writing* (ed. Denise Riley), *Scripsi*, *Southerly*, *Sydney Morning Herald*, *The Australian Newspaper*, *The Best Australian Poems 2006* (ed. Dorothy Porter), *The Best Australian Poetry 2006* (ed. Judith Beveridge), *The New World Tattoo: The Newcastle Poetry Prize Anthology 1996*, *The Moment Made Marvellous* (ed. Tom Shapcott), *Poetry Review* (UK), *The Prague Review*, *Time's Collision with the Tongue: The Newcastle Poetry Prize Anthology 2001*, *Ulitarra* and *The Warwick Review*. Various poems have been broadcast on ABC Radio National. "The Past" contains a citation from Jonathan Galassi's translation of Eugenio Montale's 'A mia madre'. "Four Songs" with music by Jonathan Mills was first performed in the Art Gallery of New South Wales series *Writers in Recital* in 1989 and later broadcast by ABC FM.

Over the last few years I have been greatly assisted by an award of the Myer Foundation's Alan Marshall Fellowship, a residency at Yaddo, NY, an Australia Council funded residency at the B.R.Whiting Library in Rome and by other fellowships from the Literature Board of the Australia Council. My sincere thanks to these organizations for the vital assistance they have offered. My thanks too for this edition to my Australian publisher Terri-Ann White at University of Western Australia Press and my British publisher Tony Frazer at Shearsman for their support of my work.

Contents

Seeing Rain   13
Seeing Paddocks   14

Earlier Poems

Then and Now   16
Burrill Transformer   17
Four Songs
    Cheap Movies   19
    The Paddock Slope   19
    The Laboratory   20
    Portable Objects   21
Red Marine   22
February Night Song   24
Isfahan   25
Cine   26
Lecture on Focus   28
Songs and Verses   30
First Glance at a Walking Party   31
Auckland Abstracts
    Plants   33
    Picture of My Mother   34
    3   34
    Rain a study   35
Lizards   37
An Ordinary Communication   43
On the Traditional Way of Painting   45
Watching Pelicans, Mallacoota   46

Wild Bees

An Elephant's Foot   48
Grass-Parrot   50
A Patch of Grass   51
Spring Song   53
Yachts at Scotland Island   54
Walking Back from the Dam   57

A Dog Barking	60
Clouds Near Waddi	61
A Breath of Wind on a Summer Night	62
Leeches	65
Letter from America *to Antigone Kefala*	67
Letter from America *to Ruark Lewis*	71
Scenic Mode	76
The Coolamon	78
Fine Rain at Night	80
A Month in the Country	81
Forest Kingfisher	84
The Witnesses	86
Sydney Lawyer with Horses	88
The Red Gum	90
Stopping for a Walk in Reserved Land Near Murra Murra	92
Remembering Floodwater	95
The Platypus	97
Tasmania	99
A Word	101
Rainbow Snake	102
Close-Ups:	
Waking	103
Roadside Near Hillston	104
The Andes	105
Tasmanian Tiger	108
A Studio in Prague	110
Late Western Thought	112
Letter from America	114
Summer	117
Night's Paddock	120

Music

Double Movement	121
Fence Posts	123
Breakfast	126
Bronzewings with Lightning	130
The Past	135
About Balance	138

The Driver	144
Winter Solstice	146
Now	151
Plum Trees	154
Paddock at Yengo	155
Suddenly, Trees	157
The Dam	159
Index of first lines	162

Preface

Not many of these Wild Bees will be known to British or American readers. With a few exceptions, it culls from books published in Australia after 1993, *The Distribution of Voice*, *The Kangaroo Farm* and *Summer*. Inevitably the selection reflects where I am heading now as much as where I have been. There are ten previously uncollected poems and the pieces from a 2005 chapbook *Music: Prose and Poems*. Perhaps, taken overall, this single book is the book I always meant to write over the last decade and a half. My poetry is described by reviewers and critics as to do with seeing and the senses, with momentariness, with the integration of things in a world of change and flux—and that account has often seemed appropriate. It is a delight too when readers take pleasure in the recognition of the poetry's local circumstances since I think that, in the main, we make local paths wherever we are. The same is true even with the most wide ranging of materials and styles. I am fortunate to have seen some of my poetry discovered by a number of ecologically conscious readers and critics who are concerned with how we live our lives environmentally, including at the most intricate and microperceptual levels of awareness. Lucky, also, to have so far escaped from being classified in a movement or a generation—new or old, innovative or formal. Finally, the limits of our experience and understanding of the world are the limits of time and of our senses, and not just of language. The provisional nature of our selves, our own temporary glimpse of the world's tragedy and loveliness, is at the heart of the matter.

M.H.

Wild Bees

Seeing Rain

A top branch shakes down
heavy rains of diamonds
while, amethyst-eyed, a silent bird
flies off among deeper leaves

After the cloud-burst this is one
can't hide in its midnight blue.
Each leap inside the cotoneaster
sputters out diamond showers.

Do bower birds see rain as I do,
glimpsing more than texture?
And what does an observer know
of pecking vermilion from the air?

Going outside, I scared it off
as if, in hiding, it could hide itself,
neither of us sensing through rain-wet light
how we divide the world with thoughts.

A top branch shakes down
heavy rains of diamonds
while, amethyst-eyed, a silent bird
flies off among deeper leaves

Seeing Paddocks

*

across the slope, emptiness like a tide sweeps everything away

*

Dry wind grazes like fire in the middle height of trees.

If there's a cloud it's in the mind not in the world.
If there's a trace or hint of it, it's a thought not a thing.
If there's an edge, it's made here along the slope.
If there's darkness, I bring it with me like blood.
If there's more darkness, it's exposed in the tree fringe.
If there's a distant zig-zag, it speeds like a snake.
It runs down the sky like an upside down tree.
If it delivers an idea of change, it hits, it strikes.
(Rain smell, memory of wetness on strewn bark litter,
sound of rain, markings of rain on the ground.)
If it strikes, it brings fire, air, water.
If it breathes, it undries the mind like waking from a dream.
If it remembers, it gives back the dream's clear outlines.
(Today no-one remembers the earth dream, the land dream.)
(Over there, a car goes silently by in its wind-river.)
If it's too hard to get back there, leaf clusters parachute down.
If you want to look, you must look in the corner.
If there's a play of shadow and untruth, bright wind still glares.
The surprised stillness of earth powders into dust.
The wind too is a leap a jump from one look to another.
If a root system drops from a swollen purple cloud.
One strike brings fire, air, water.
Three strikes brings gaol, mostly over nothings.
If you look you must look in the corner of the eye.
If there's a gash of granite boulders, the flesh clefts them.
If the breath's elements (soul elements) have dried like a dream.
(Rythmed by the fence, a car goes silently by.)
If we place death somewhere, we will start forgetting it.

If death is placed here, it will start remembering.
It happens instantly.
The wind too is a leap between two views, two looks.
If—even if—there's a dry place the past still weeps there.
When the wind trowels the sky, it leaves blue hints of thunderheads.
Over there, the paddock gazes out with its blond, bare contours.

across the slope, emptiness like a tide sweeps things away

Earlier Poems

Then and Now

Beyond the curtains, outside,
a screen of white like Finland's dusk,
an eyeblink blinding out the north:
I fall asleep, forget the frame.

Late wind arrives, shakes the leaves
in a porridge of shimmers, like a mane—
a lion gets up, walks about,
caged, foetid, in a fitful mind;

he's the lion of noise,
lion of cricket-clinking moons
which rise, sharp as ice,
through sea-like blue behind a ridge.

Overhead, night's a black cockatoo,
mind's pattern dancing among its toys.
Nearby, where the slope's streaked with head-lights,
shadowy, red harvesters grind up and down.

Burrill Transformer

A clear stillness hangs in the cormorant's cry,
limpid as a phial of water, stark as bare magnolias.
Behind us headlands flash from where we lay,
out across white dunes. By now, those hollows
will have cooled down, dented with purple light.
There, grass-spikes shiver against the surf's blur.
Overhead, dusk-sky shifts round, sprouting its
cabbage-row of evening clouds, along the sea's edge.
Distant, a cattle truck rattles on the causeway,
moving like a target, past the spilt tide's
mix of mercury and frozen mirror. Watching it
we stop a while to take the lake's dimensions in,
both floods and barriers: on the other side,
casuarinas, at water level, shine from their vantage point
freshly acquiring cream-gauzed, fuzzy sprays—
their ragged boughs are now picked out
beyond the low sun's water track. You understand it,
turning round, wind-scarfed, walking by me—
you cannot help be blinded by this change
as if, in pure occurrence, a sound rings out.
Do you remember, earlier, someone drawing a curtain
in the fibro house next door? Do you remember
how you heard it? As a further noise,
back of the mouth's cry, made of
rough guesswork from thought to thought, imagining
how strangeness can emerge from dying love.
That love was held in breathless, light-fleshed groans:
a dark blue rippling among the estuary's muddy shine.

This is why the dusk swarms up, unseen, saturated,
where cicadas switch on their background roar,
as in a waterfall heard so intently
it seems fixed, dazzling, in the ear. It's why too
it seems we're standing now on a high-rise balcony,
looking down at people crossing at lights:

they're just night's soldier-crabs scuttling at our feet.
Wet things, glinting, under a water-film.
Only coolness arrives in this profuse sense,
starting its slow transforming act,
its silence like a shimmer in the air.
That bluish tinge now separates out, is gone.
Each way we turn, a sediment must fall
in a down-drifting, powdery storm,
anything to stop the onset of the stars' pinprick net
in whose clear medium, nearly back home, we move.

Four Songs

1. Cheap Movies

In winter dusk, a mindless sea.
A rear-view mirror filled with red—
it's like a 50s cinema screen,
before the film begins. Late wind

shakes the car, blows the waves, flutters
torn wrappers in the rubbish cans.
The bushes suddenly are tipped with chrome,
the grass turns grey as unwashed wool.

Out there, it's going on, a change
from blue to deeper blue and grey—
the cormorant tracking over water
looks like a hair across a lens.

The sea returns as jolting light,
surf-noise rolling towards the cliffs.
No moon tonight. Just a wave's whiteness,
like leaping grains on an old print.

2. The Paddock Slope

Saplings run down the slope like girls. Blue-grey,
they have escaped into the paddock.
Now like a spring flood, they stand both sides
of the fence. To someone on a survey,

they're a spur, a corner of bush left behind,
re-growth, darting, like a lizard's tongue.
Stubbled with round-topped stones, the land greets the horse:
here, too, a stick could paint it on a shield.

Within these things, unfathomed sea hangs fire,
journeys away yet more than depth.
Chains of cattle cross in paddock haze,
under midday's dome, blue as thought. The wire-

fence hems in an unaxed stand. There's a sense
everywhere of dry grass fading, seeding. The map's as thin
as an old man's sparse blond hair,
where wives and husbands start their ends.

3. The Laboratory

Dying, a ragged measure, across a ridge
the last flare of orange goes
into a shining plain of water:
black-etched sky. Moth-flecks are flowers.

The dusk's blue was like a wind,
soon gone, soon settled, before night.
Now grass lengthens into streaks of ice,
while, bigger than a torch, full moon

rises from nowhere, reaching flood,
making the tree-stumps jump like rabbits,
re-drawing the tangled orchard's branches
into a nest of wires, and flickering leaves.

Owls murmur, star-vines start to trail.
A nearby tractor, cooling, sets up its tick.
Car-lights probe and pass along the fence,
glancing at hard, new fruit. Untasted yet.

4. Portable Objects

Up here in the plum-tree's wands,
the smell of fruit and cooler air:
it's an old photo, quite old.
A young man, snapped, is laughing there.

The photo lies inside a drawer,
opened, half-jammed, for something else:
car keys, lost numbers, a swirl of stars.
Things burn like matches in this quiet house.

There he is, a boy's face in twigs,
too young to know how light is hard.
Yellow fruit's picked before it's ripe.
A clock face shines in laurel shade.

Time's held in mind against that tree,
the ridge's slope has got torn off.
Like pearl-grey lakes, far orchards glint:
boxed up, old letters gather love.

Red Marine

The meaning of that movement must be found
in the collapsing schema of red sails,
though it happened out there, in dwindling light,
upon the edge, half-seen, a mere detail.

More total, more for the body than the eye,
it turned dusk's wind into a flapping hinge
while the gulls, alarmed, skimmed up across the bay,
suddenly caught in white again, wheeling

seawards, changing places in a relay,
until their veering made a dream of depth:
blind memory rising in a flickering wave.
(Its house is death. Its window is a hearth.)

It was as if, just then, a river shone,
as if, behind that wave, lost voices spoke—
voices heard after they had gone away.
The burden left is trivial, instant, black.

And yet you see that movement as it is,
crossing, like tide itself, through mobile space:
on the sea edge a sail topples, a red
tulip-flame twists in wind. The bright sea's

glitter, with people bobbing in it, swallows it up
like interference blizzarding a screen.
There was a moment of cloud shadow, more
nostalgic than squint-eyed, orange sun

where fixed, half-noticed things remain as glints,
leaving behind them latency in time,
a spectral body stretched from shore to shore,
gulls in perspective, spindrifts of white sperm.

A sailboard's red sail folds into the sea,
no substitute for fictions of a mind
which searches an exacter entity
in blind, green light over the harbour's tomb.

February Night Song

You, the world, the house,
but tonight you're not happy.
No-one can sleep this month.
Across the park, the lights are sultry.

So we lie in our dark bed,
naked on a blue sheet,
under shadowy indoor plants—
we're woken by the clock, the street.

Outlined in the buzz of haze
your dancer's body:
still half-awake I categorise
your alarm of self and place.

For when at last we turn to sleep
in the end of summer dark,
I'll see you as the white heron
flapping wings of glittering water.

Isfahan

That half-open amber eye fixed on you,
the woman in the kitchen half turning to you—
drowsy tonight, you take in the angles
of chairs, walls, old photos, a painted vase.

There, a heron's stillness helps it vanish,
wading by a wind-flecked lake.
Outside, car-noise glistening after early rain.
Night's silence builds its inner ear.

So birds croak from a cracked, green bush,
the mouth's distortion roars into an amulet,
but nothing distinguishes each memory,
solidified into a white-domed zone:

a set of blocks along a slope, a fossil trace,
kitchen clatter acquires a blinder shape.
Its time is ridged like wind-blown sea.
Suddenly lit up, cat's-eyes down a moonless road.

Cine

The shirtless young
man pushes (blue tint,

brown) a hand back
over his beard:

and with the other,
steers a lawnmower

over the strip,
stones sputtering.

I film his stride
thighwards, in sun

on broad shoulder-muscle
linked to the handle:

his pale jeans
dinted by light.

His shout's roundness
is as shiny as

a car top which
repeats his eye

and bareburnt
surface—his

elbow thrust
skims at grass.

There, shadow is
his white's humour:

his sportshoes measure
the lawn's growth.

Getting lost in
an uncut patch as

later (now carrying a
filled hutch) he

enters the gully,
snaps off withes

of still pink-laden
springy oleanders

with an upswing
throw that goes

outwards in a
pelt of pebbles,

ruck of clippings.
That green cloud is

thrown into the branches
like rain dripping—

next, his hand returns
so that he may

steady his heel's
glinting catch.

Lecture on Focus

All water is dusk, or light blenched. A mauve shade,
some water is so large it fills up the lens,
becoming mere thought occurring here or there
as if in a place which was chosen for it,
on a surface, in a container, inside an edge.

Close-up, green bars of water greet an eye blinking
as it turns transparent, partial, on moving skin.
Here a body lunges on, diminishing, in shocks.
Some water is a mask, the cover of a cave
which has no walls and which flows, unawares,

round points, indentations, grooves, visages.
Surfacing faces look out like people in a car
which has braked, swinging round, in a crash.
Other are caught wading, motionless like stilts,
while a lozenge shaped launch lifts in swayed water.

But the water is silent, browsing on itself:
only its frontiers are audible events,
as in weed-suck and rock's knife-cuts,
with a mechanism of hands and arms heaving
through it to striped buoys at eye-level.

One side you find dark patches, a house's old mirrors,
tarnished by salt wind. Midway, a white post soars—
the water swells past it, glistening, breathing,
as expectantly as a birthday child at table.
Further on, elbows flash from one blue ridge to the next.

What is it here which moves too bright to see,
like a mob of galahs, plummeting from a branch
into wispy, mud-cracked stubble? What moves in multiples,
consistent, winged, making involuntary
structures out of scattered, minimal beats?

It is water. Water under dryness. A plain of light,
now a series of retreating fringes,
or flanges perhaps, like a cloth held over a fire
which burns through at several points
and thus reshapes itself. First a net,

(the swimmer pulls himself through its white flame),
then a kind of membrane folding back and up
which twists out new slopes, connected hill sides,
of itself: dazzled ocean floods the mind's tombs,
linking them like shots framed in sleep.—

It's a dream sped up to unseeable quickness.
It's the kind of dream which a sleeper wakes from
recalling only a tone, or the muffled flight
of a thing, not the scene or the face's meaning—
whatever words there were slip by like a forward

darting glance-wise to the touch. You focus again:
sea-lion clouds peer up over a ragged ledge,
part of a cliff line which has no time for colour.
The place is now mandala, now perhaps montage,
where a bed explodes in its cauldron of ripples,

themselves suggesting a fish's back sliding under,
or a shoulder curving through sculpted cups,
or water becoming dusk, or light blenched.

Songs and Verses

The white table, the white chairs,
there under the casuarinas—
flies circle it, buzzing, zig-zagging:
the eye's blood-red cotton vein.

*

Back there, a small room's packed up life:
silence reigns in this house. Street-sounds
wash in like ripples, lapping a fallen log.
Beyond them, tree-clouded lakes murmur.

*

We are on a journey,
a journey which is ours,
made of figurative moves
asking who made so many souls.

The journey goes on,
though you and I stay still:
mosquitoes swarm the dried-up creeks,
ghostly herons stalk bronze reeds.

*

Here a grub hammers away
at its world of sky and wood:
there's day sheen, there's day glimmer,
while warm gusts glint on bark.

First Glance at a Walking Party, Barrington Tops ca. 1895

As in a photograph by a small town artist
regional, unknown, whose sepia wandering work
fetches up in libraries as support
against myth-made progeniture, or, as here,
is caught again in April's stencil work glinting
against the wood panels of a tourist lodge,

there's more to its choice than just the eye.
What the eye sees, plate glassed or not, is mostly learnt.
A leaf-rustled, bellbird solitude calls to them,
they whose sense, togged up, was of getting-far,
never the first time quite, yet intending a newness
raw as sawn log ends, timely as a wheel's sprayed sand.

Held under breath, their words are dark ice-blue
like a pool flooded with late, upland snow—
you see their long-awaiting, intense eyes,
fixed in a spacious, brown-varnished frame. Looking back,
we're watched, fresh-faced by spivvy, statuesque
men in ribboned boaters, and crushed Panamas, and by plump

middle-aged women, firm-necked in pleated tweeds:
only the youths have that hair-parted look,
modern, steadfast, self-conscious,
soon able to fly planes, or pick up the telephone.
Front left, someone's tulle-bloused daughter,
fulsomely caught between home life and an idea,

stares out past our future—being perhaps the
same age as my wife's grandmother, "first female student
at London's Slade", whose own Victorian mother transported
thirty portmanteaux through far-flung vicarage worlds,
looping Jamaica, Teneriffe, India, out to here.
This photo, though, tells nothing of unlikely

provenance, back of flower arrangements, deathly memorials,
or last-minute wills bequeathing razored paddocks.
A cloudy stillness, a hand nervously blurring,
deprive them of a lack of origin,
some of them dressed in graziers' touring duds
but all of them defined in a balletic idiom

of bird and breath, of cream-gauze sun-up
intently glowering on a wire. In their minds' Sydney,
blue-brick memories, hazy, pinnacled, flow
into a glance, carrying out its introduction—
a thing soon checked by polished boots, starched collars,
heads askance with Ma and Pa. So, they wait.

They wait in order to recall themselves—
glazed, shimmering, like lakeside reeds—
within a glittering transformation, a beatitude,
now about to exit in a photograph,
shining like the bush's cut-out veins of light.
Dated, they'll walk away by car and telegram.

Caught in this rainy air, they're indelibly faded
on a rucked-up backdrop of negroheads,
conjoined warlike among 19th Century
parsonage sounds, about to break ranks and stretch their legs,
till they glimpse our future mood loading up the Commodore—
towels, camp-smoke, Ampol, bursts of shellac-bouncing sun.

Auckland Abstracts

1. Plants

There's already a fishing boat just moved out from behind a spur of trees. Over there, a whole spray of numerals, a calculation of names.

*

Darkness "wound down" / the sun's partial climb over wires and a thread-line of clouds and the abstraction of farms complete my dream, my walk and the pattern of numbers

*

A bird flies off with a rustle of black silk over Edwardian ferns—but what's surprising is the compactness of the dark-painted wooden house under its silver roof and cream verandah—how quiet and "finished" the whole scene.

*

A sound of a hammer, a mower, a car revving; the noise of the sun veering round into position—one of the slowest bodily cycles, plectral, triangular—but there's a tremendous striving to take up maximum angle.

*

Littering the pathway, a tricycle the emptiness which happens to live between heart and lungs
People in sheer desperation "the worst" "the best"

*

ANNABELLES Bon Soir Paree YOUR FATHERS MOUSTACHE The Coleman Sound HEIDELBERG ROOM Bobby Davis ACE OF CLUBS Lil's Palace of Varieties OLIVERS CHANGING TIMES The Company

*

Chair moving on the verandah, rocking backwards and forwards as the very fair-haired child goes back to the door's shadow of sharp vermilion.—Next to it there's a pair of shoes, left behind for reasons of spirit

2. Picture of My Mother

Some days some voices
the room musty like a compartment in an old 50's train
I remember a totally different childhood
each day working my way through rain a few words
whatever's sentient articulates my own hand
my tongue speaks in this way a river of images to the window my hand
        holds
stand by the window! birdswing catapult
a glowing picnic among the cedars
small brick terraces overshadowed by the gigantic legs of pylons
shall I photograph you or simply imagine dance-like movements?
since the motors freezing in snow are invaded by the still grove
they locked up the foundry in your grandfather's day
some day, he muttered, to be automatic on and composed of moors
to lose that language which is universal and unites all persons
from this simple tuft I look back at you as you stand by one of the arches
        of the stone-built viaduct

3.

Dear Steve,

I imagine you are now sitting in the lotus position on the balcony in front of W's house.

I don't know whether your eyes are open or whether you've had them closed for several minutes in order to see better the valley in front of you. Myself I see there the slopes of trees, a grey cloud, an estuary making a hollow among the bordering hills. Perhaps your eyes are open because it's too hard to delimit anyone's head, as it flows between natural events. So that I easily believe in light scratch marks on the tide's surface whose centre isn't a mirror, has no frame: I don't mean a record, a vibration, no storage system for utterable extents of feeling. Love. Birds. Mouths. Taking off as they do from infinite points to glide | *water* which is green flowing in perspective with all the landmarks measured out as strictly as worktime in factories

4. Rain *a study*

I move to them, vertical rivers waking up with a few words (only the opening) in my head and it's pouring with rain in the way it's tended to do a lot after daybreak stillness in grey light in the house's two rooms and I'm half dreaming of green strings of rain through all the delicate leaves, on the furniture and melting the flowers. Up above, its tuneless noise spreads a terrific impetus, layers and cascades of it outside down to the earth dawnlight growing, taut slopes of your body lie under me

beak of rain

*

Later

The jug stays quietly in the shelf's darkness. A fire burns through the layer of coal which had been built up earlier. A condensation of concern, its remaining love for another, is hidden in unnoticeable gestures, as bread too is put away in a clay container to keep it from the onroads of ants. Night has brought a sidelong glance in which we're seen as beings threaded on a wire: it's in the aspiration of such a narrow edge offered to each other that we have hopes, love each other.

Alone our eyes like cut flowers leaning from a vase remember the mauve sheets of the morning's unmade bed

Lizards
for Sylvia Lawson

Quick as the shutter noise
clicking behind a lens
the lizards dart out
on the plain, warm surface

of the back wall outside
the kitchen. They hang there,
idly floating up, like spacemen
clambering outwards from their ship.

Or they scutter rattling
along a crevice
as if they hurtle to and fro
inside a groove: nervy things,

cousins of snake and mice,
they dash for cover under
a net of flickering leaves,
which light snaps on and off. This

is where they live. Winter
flashes over them, making
their necks swivel, making
the bricks under them as white

as burning sun. Such change
mimics their marks. A tail
curves in an imaginary
swerve of escape

which ends with the squiggle
of a cool body, half-frozen
on a camouflaged area,
perhaps a close-up of bare branches,

a dissolve to trees. This
moment, they're not here,
or are merely playing
at being silhouettes, quite still.

The next, one of them skitters
far off like a boy
running out of bounds in
a game of tag. Maybe

the sun shouts after it,
quickens its pulse, tempting it
out of the dusty cranny
where it poses, waiting.

Back again, they're like
cut-outs,
marionettes of stop and go,
acting the danger-stripes down

their flanks, as they manoeuvre
with each other. Anyone would think
they could fall upwards,
suspended on this wall

which they flick over with
spread surfies' toes. Other times,
timidly they let themselves
be flattened out, thin

as layers of earth or
stone, a section for the eye
to light on: where a kestrel might
hover over, swoop, then pounce.

*

You asked me once about
a poem—its power
to change a world and, as
an icon, rule all images.

Yet the poem, a poem is
not that active. It, too,
converts
verticals into horizontals,

taking a lizard's eye,
its brazen mind of cloud.
Here, each place becomes
a screen, and the crimson

of new rose-shoots gets
that flicker-effect
you find in old movies:
partly it's decayed celluloid,

partly the speed of frames
which strike past, visibly.
Like skinks, lurking movements
are composed. They hide and show.

Things which are picked out
in a moment's glance
become a play of squares,
a play of stance and gaze

to be included, left aside,
just remembered in the way
you catch a nearby branch,
wind-pleated, in today's crowd,

while the place which the eye takes
goes dark along its edge—
an absence filled with longing,
nervous, expectant.

It's like the wish to be loved,
turning into sexual sadness.
Each moment, it's as if
a sea draws back,

conscious, behind
your shoulder, leaving
a beach of sloping skin, a litter
of stony blurs and shells.

Now the lizards' cross-hatch marks
become tracks in a desert
which a plane, high up,
crawls over, its shadow a pointer.

The traveller hangs in air
censoring where he is:
a surface gaze whose
half-seen lizards dart in light.

Movement mimics motion.
The art of our time—
words shoot through like arrows,
or fix things on a map

of our own making,
our own cause.
The branch, the tree, the wall
wavers. Skinks, run away.

*

But they don't. They stay.
And someone
walks out of a house
into his yard filled with sun,

his mind fogged with
afternoon TV
whose floating colours figure out
a greenish map of dots and stripes—

he finds these lizards
skittering on the wall,
like handmarks
or ritual objects spread on sand: a kind

of flashback, perhaps a photo
in an album,
looking out at rocks and outlined people,
scattered in the mulga brush.

What occurs
is complex here, because
the man is cut by what he is,
by where he looks—as if a camera

shoots his view. His thoughts
are filled with news,
traces, the quivering
things which build these running forms

into a tenuous net
of lit-up words. Once more, lizards dart
upon dark skin
and pattern what the world will say:

now he is thinking
of space, like a
hand-held shield, mobile with stars
and stony tracks. Now, of them.

An Ordinary Communication

About the yard, about warm air
floating with bell-like sounds,

about things becoming bells
and tones and long-drawn-out noise,

about that vulnerable point with
enough reach, enough touch,

so that things which are sounds
fall, like fruit with wasps around it,

out of leaf-littering trees,
and can be felt as tracks—

as spaces crossed by moths
uprising in a cloud—

about these things you have to find
an imagery of holes,

of points which, effortlessly, hover
on a screen, or of woven

twigs: a torn T-shirt, a
terminal, a nest. These

are oddities of mind's routine,
part of a dance—

a kite riding yesterday's wind,
crackling, inexplicable—

where movements make themselves
other than as they are:

metaphors in music,
substantial as the yard.

It could be cloth burnt through,
a painted canvas, a string-bag.

This, then, is translation
out of ordinary space—

not word for word,
but as someone might feel

sitting outside, in dusklight,
hearing bells and traffic,

hearing the shrubs quiver
their bright, red filaments,

a window closing next door
rattling down like a hail-shower,

suddenly gone. But he keeps on
waiting there, in whitest, final air.

On the Traditional Way of Painting

A sea-leaf is laid across the bark:
I've given up talking
save through the world as it is.

But the leaf is no philosopher.
It's just an edge, a flare-mark,
and not a thing in itself.

The light moves in with the colours which it gives,
it's used here as an instrument
in a pattern of camouflaged stones.

Here I see the way I walk,
here I become the shadow,
the bleached crab-shell among pebbles,

and I notice how a thin sheet of rock slants into the sun.
Everyone lives and hunts and fishes,
everyone lives and is well.

A hot wind bursts in my face and round my neck,
drowning out the glare of the beach's multi-coloured shells.
Blue surf topples under the ledges of my ears.

Like fire in a grate the flicker of the sea-wrack's leaf—
while the red-daubed wooden fish clack against each other
with bark twine threaded through their tails.

Watching Pelicans, Mallacoota

A she-oak needle glitters at midday,
a point, a thing in equilibrium.
It's like a mark, overexposed,
in a photo—or a white cell burning
with the pottery glaze of daybreak's remnant moon.
The needle flickers like bunting in a used-car yard.
It glitters like foil, being too piercing
to gaze at unless you catch it as you pass,
or, half-squinting, let it flash. In this, it
strikes right home—it has an aura,
a feel, by which it's magnified. The needle
shimmers. Its white fire's now remembered
as the linen whiteness of a long-lived sickness,
which, intervening just as
you did not want it, tragically opens life up
leaving you later with mere sickness-at-heart—
too much whiteness, too much intensity,
fading, going for nothing. This, though, is the white glare
of fever and snow—nothing to do with she-oaks.

A glitter reaches out, expires, resides,
acquiring future, being no migratory thing—
no virus splitting, dumbstruck, in a microscope.
Here, nothing prepares you for the she-oak's shining
or the dazzle spilt along the water's purple track,
when, exactly at that moment, you watch the pelican touch down
with a clumsy skate, a half-crumpled splash,
its web-foot ambers submitting to its whites:

awkward and beautiful,
the bird sorts itself out, preening and pecking
its half-flapped wings, shaking a throat
of empty sagging skin, wrinkled like a scrotum's,
before it floats glassily away
to an out-of-reach patch, beyond the she-oak,

where pink-toned the bending surface runs darker, more mellow.
It swims off, in perspective almost a swan,
unperplexed by its gawky fall from grace,
able at will to hang in the estuary's gusts,
sustained by the ribbed, white blur
it casts on the water's sheen—
that blur is like the body's memory gain,
a nerve-end coming back, having its drift defined
in fractured awareness of a bird through rippling light,
while, lost to view, the near-by she-oak needle winks at empty air.

# Wild Bees

An Elephant's Foot

No cool place on the verandah
and, once again, the half-thought of fire:
even the metal ticks under the heat's weight.
In trees, up the back, cicadas are noisy
as electricity in a transformer.

They burn through you, can't be avoided.
They're too close on the ear, too amplified.
Thousands of them hiss from the slope.
They buzz non-stop like a jammed CD.
Occasionally, one close-by sprays out

its clicks, mid-pitched, a barber's shaver
(trimming sideburns) on the skull; while way over
the predicted top, the heat's now powering up
its empty hot-plate—its main purpose being
erasure of depth, to be a destroyer

of whatever's peripheral and delicate,
as totally as an elephant's foot. By
mid-morning, the temperature's a blood storm,
one signal (there are hundreds) of life-change
in the way trunks, branches, even grass-stalks

have got glued with tiny, wrecked mandibles
and paper car-bodies. Black Princes, Yellow
Bakers, Greengrocers keep unzipping from them,
flying off, giving 40° its voice;
till they throb an ear-splitting, dry sea-swell

raking long messages through heat
no-one can be out in—rasping more consonants
and Bushman clicks than an ear absorbs,
flittering out to an insect-horizon
whose sounds blaze, build, then counterpoint

in a chorus of football fans who chant
and sing across a stadium. It's said
these sound-curtains can bring on heart-attacks.
They take over, stimulate the pulse too much;
they make environment. In fact, though, who was it

invented the phrase 'wall of sound'? Containment
is practised first in the ear, in what you trust;
then in unheard voices no-one resists.
It's why, for a second, a stray temptation
about how, in town, the supermarket's

corridors of packaged goods stay cooled
nudges into mind like an absent wisp of cloud:
fresh passages, cold hums, cool music float
on a surface whose deep features can't be tracked
consciously—a transparent fire-front lodged

in the cicada-air. No choice but to take
it on, be philosophical, or make
humour out of these shadowy desires
even for air-con, for shade, for surf;
after all, a phase where singularity's unmarked

in an immersion of machine-noised air
is one where *is* and *was,* like ripples of
water, die on arrival. Noise is always
more complex than speech. Cicadas blast voll-
eys. They're precise. They deny transcendence.

Grass-Parrot

Two days later, I see again
long hectares of white plains bristling
the other side of the road's verge:
blue marks flitter, opal showers flash,
becoming grass-parrots which leap up
from bleached waist-high grass, then back again
in tiny rocking-horse movements
of springing curves and perfect falls.
Foraging, they twitter a hundred miles.
Out there, heat-blurred across paddock glare,
dark trees float along the horizon's line:
bushes are wallabies, swivelling their ears.
Through my hair, hot wind's flooded creek.

Cloudless sky moves, without seeming to,
in an eye-blink over the Silver City Highway.

A Patch of Grass

The dark green, the light green,
the pale native rosemary flowers,
blue-grey like low rain clouds,
and, behind them, an intense spiked green
of boronia, seed-heads, meadow-grass,
thistles and thistle-heads—
a slope of them, a scarred bank,
held down by agapanthus clumps,
rambling grevillea, more boronia:

patches of bare, hard clay
exposed where the sun burns out the
surface, or where little run-offs
stop the grass from taking, offer a
tattered shawl of thin weeds, spires of fireweed,
a kind of parsley, twigs,
bark-litter from a gum-tree,
and the bake of a harsh, blue sky
reflected in quartz-hued

pebbles, a sandstone rock
not too heavy to lift, dwarf-sized
escarpments waving with
shell grass, dandelions, small groundsels
also flowering. There are slender violets,
too, which I thought had been
introduced, but I looked them
up: they're native—two-toned, purple
and pale mauve (like lilac)

interlaced with chickweed
and couch grass. The land slopes somewhat
there, giving that chance
of openness which some species need
as well as the chance of dead erosion

by rain, by heat which splits
earth—I mean, by motion
of soils as natural as the shifts
which hollow out slow changes

in any body tak-
ing on contours of age and use.
Taking on more, it's a
place for everything, allowing an
instant of transformation—of wildness—
as a registering
of greenness beyond the eye's
capacity (what does it see?) to
grade green as straw-coloured,

verdant, or shadowed. A
green re-mapped by swirls of firetails
on a seed-search. In such
half-seeing of the world, it's the bird's-
eye view which makes the tangle into a
fixed space for words, adding
once more that hint of pale
rainy blue, shimmering beneath
the network of grasses:

a phrase like "everything's
place" might be appropriate to this
lingering gaze—though that's
to say, "lost to its people," "no long-
er mantic," "not named in speech." Small patch
of earth. It stays like this
until you understand it
as light, unconscious flesh; and it
becomes you, as you it.

Spring Song

Its odd system knows something we don't.
Lucky, then, that our air-dropped swallows did,
moving house from the back, starting drab mud-cornices
along the front verandah, taking a chance.

Out of nowhere, they'd come back to *la niña's* cold wedge.
Over our heads, coastal weathers, icy inland dries,
fought it out invisibly like a stock-market war,
like a play of digits, a group-force running through.

Their shimmers were the bent light of holograms
as they screeched, flickering, under the tin roof
in a behaviour which looked random, landing on a ledge,
then on the rail. Hovering. Uncertain. Shifting place.

They checked and changed with what was still unseen,
building a pocket inside the land's transparency.
Its record-breaking mood surrounded them with cool
and programmed them, like sleep, to guess its drift.

In one week's blue loop, they modelled no-thought, void, *nada*.
Again and again they skimmed through that same place where
a driver (screaming at it) misses a car, or a nerve-end throbs,
or where the flame-tree, by the gate, smoulders up with fire.

Yachts at Scotland Island
for Marcia Stewart

After a day of Greek references, lunch, and Freudian puns
the *mythoi* aren't appropriate to the dapple and sting-rays
any more than to a brain verbalising everlastingly
on its right-side stones and its left-side waters. But, no less,

the TV, modernity's end, the abolition of craft in networks—
all those roadways through intelligent starlit places—
are short meeting-spaces with cartoon characters
hanging in trees, or just the other side of the bay.

I go to Soundsite, Leonardo, Fanzine and MLA.
Outside, water noise ripples in flickering rosemary bushes.
Inside, the modem chatters in its own drifting sky.
Sometimes it's a frog by a creek. My hand glides with its mouse.

Smart theorists, like hang-gliders, call this sensory geography
which maps travel through the texts which build it, a place
of fire in which the passageways are infinite yet framed.
There's no closeness. Or too much. A pack of cards, a street vanishes.

Appliances are light and portable. You need nothing.
Not just the heat, you dress in sleeveless shirts and go barefoot.
Even to work is to study fragments which are locked, submarine,
and the air's cinematic forest jangles its symbols of light—

while, incessantly, new worlds tempt you with patched-up bits,
floating in a medium less real than water. Names are tags,
which once were metaphors, for views down the road,
for the boss, for the book or the sea: or rather, for rags

weightlessly falling as in the last scene in that Antonioni movie,
where the whole house explodes like a flight of birds.
What's left is its owner's first risky choice, a Mojave Desert view.
In the film, it's the desert which gives the sense of distant clouds.

Myself, too, I usually work my best away from water.
I prefer it as one element among dry-country scapes
which here only the pathway's European rosemary reminds me of—
like a mallee sunset over a plain of yellow-flowering rape

whose sharp, flat skyline becomes a shimmering lake and burns,
or, air-borne, like the sense that an ancient tide's exposed the Olgas,
sculpted by sand storms and the air's weight. Residues which repeat,
this use of drifting, underwater images is a sign of our times:

that is, until a slow-building change occurs towards mid-afternoon,
shifting the glare in the grey gum overhanging the verandah
and spilling out pale blue hammerheads over blunt, green slopes.
Perhaps I get up to close the windows. Somewhere, a minah-

bird starts to fret. There's a tropical stillness. Then branches move.
Briny, the heat comes on moody, heavy, grey as a porpoise,
inclining the yachts in leeward wind as if they're random shapes,
abstract triangles like styrofoam chips, fleeting, behind glass:

you see them caught in a bar of choppy wavelets—it's like a wedge—
or frozen on a water-shelf, dark as the Sargasso's and as strange.
Now, as the wind whips up, they make their way to the channel,
where the ocean they engrave slops about in a white meringue.

It was Plato (that dramatist) who first distinguished place from space,
granting the latter its deathly power of giving, mapping, taking away,
imagining it as a sieve sifting the threshed Just-Nows—
a wall of brightness landing across stormy, green-chipped wakes,

or a fruitful, black bulb of laden sea-cloud about to burst its charge.
The yachts sail away under it like ducks gliding on a shooting-range.
Conscious of the change, I shift the pointers on the flowing screen
and log instructions for a letter which needs ten seconds to Brisbane,

half-catching only the suspense of the quick, unnoticed tuning
by which the wind's simplest shiver across the grey gum is a voice,
still whispering as it once did: Yes, I wait at the known world's pillars.
Or: A boat of flowers bearing you, I am the old man's winnow.

Walking Back from the Dam

It leaves in my eyes the image of a
pearl-grey lake fleshed with blue, rain-clearing clouds,
the awakening scent of rain-wet grass, sharpness of
amber light through a clump of swamp mahoganies;
brighter than an hour back, it's dusk after
a day of steady, soaking falls ("no-one
can complain," the guy in the store tells me
earlier on.) Good weather floating through,
front after front, from the west.
                              In this pause,
swallows, scissoring fifty feet above,
skirt across the neighbour's paddocks. They're like
sheepdogs rounding up an invisible,
panicking flock—insect-sheep which never
form a mob or head to the gate. So the swallows
fly round and round, swerving, turning in air
which is still and lucid. They vanish, crossing
like space-probes before the sun, flickering, zipping,
in a backwards and forwards tennis-match;
while under the swamp mahoganies, that amber glow
settles ochre puddles across bare ground.
Then they're back again, working the area,
but now it's like they're picking threads from off a cloth.
It's that dense, this thick, this feeling of time—
this feeling of walking back alone under
the trees. As if somehow, the whole world's in
another tense. Or as if you could still be young,
striding back, shadow-flinging, across the grass
in light sharp as a knife-blade, pools of it.

I've neighbours never moved away from here.
They're what's left, when a place is just enough:
a family, a house, the sister moves in too—
with a first child after the husband's baled out.
They're one side. Down the road, an ex-muso

and his wife—both out of work though perhaps
they live on savings anyhow. Sometimes I hear
them shouting at their dogs. Otherwise, there
are these moments, never quite catchable,
which could trick you into thinking "This
is how it is, this is the way things always look."
Like a swirl in a flooded creek, the braid
of things is plaited tight, floating, moving,
never repeating the same glitter, the
same hillock of twisting water. Nothing, in short,
which would not be particular—and tricksy,
addictive, not to be too much believed. For that's
the killer: there is so much already gone through—
'so many star-shows since the 70s'—
making it possible to read back the stages
of anybody's life, here, today. So much
life, too much of it: detritus, memory, phrases.
(I live, I'd say, in the age of biography.)

Holed up by a day of rain now the long dry spell's
ended at last, I've been reading Ian Hamilton's
engaged "period-study" of Robert Lowell—
American, private-incomed—who made his work
bigger than life, his own life monstrous with
its breakdowns, after winter, every year:
manic depression, lithium, mornings started up
with vodka and milk, students, protest-readings,
Harvard, Italy, London, chain-smoking
and partying, carrying that mix
of aggression and weakness so attractive
to women. It hooks in. It brings nostalgia
for an older generation I knew back then—
who wanted their everyday life to perform
a universal act, a freedom out of politics.
It seems another world, a rich world gone today.

No-one stopped drinking, working only
on vacation (six months) whether in Maine or Suffolk.
Back in New York, you could die in taxis.
Fame, too, was serious, personal, mythic:
an image captioned in the heart of things.
As if you lived, hovering, in the sun's eye. And
when it was sunset, there was Rome and cocktails.
Everyone met everyone—stuck, anxious,
suicidal—dreaming themselves, frantically, to death.

A Dog Barking

Some things are beyond talking.
Not the mind, not emotions,
words will always come for them.
Perhaps the mind lives in this barrier
entirely of its own creating. You
see it the way it is, it looks back the same.—
The fence, the lake, they're just there.

Some things, though, can't be spoken.
I don't mean sex or family strife
which, fast enough, have silent words, their looks
black as emptiness through the kitchen-door
at night. Sex, anxiety, secrets—
that's what stays hidden when the wife's
still washing up from tea and her husband

stomps off to bed. It's money really,
or too much work, brings them down.
While the thing which is beyond talking
is beyond their strangeness too.
What's left unsaid is mostly what is known,
a dog barking, embers when the sun sets,
a tree's late apples stained a deeper red.

That, too, isn't much to say. The wording
of anger, fearsomeness, family ghosts
drowns the brain in its non-stop TV.
Neurones buffer up like dodgem cars.
Birds swoop down through invisible nets.
But something suddenly must rescue you:
the darkness of crickets trilling, shining.

Clouds Near Waddi

On looking up at the elephants
you could wonder where you were
for they were hovering on a chain
like Hannibal's in the Alps—

elephant shapes, bulging, linked together
crossing from north to south,
visible as a desert fantasy
of warnings, pillars, God's truth.

White narcissi, they came from nowhere
along the edge like sky's debris,
intruders in another medium
like stage scenery painted on that blue,

painted so you forgot Springtime hordes
of yellow daisies conquering new wheat,
or Paterson's Curse in purple ribbons
flickering either side of the road

and forgot those huge Egyptian prows
unmoored, two days back, amid green—
the Grampians, Mt Arapiles
drifting on the Wimmera's plain.

For, as I drove, earth was paradox,
flat for miles yet curving into clouds—
sensed like a rear-view mirror's glimpse
yet always opening up, leading onwards,

through skylines' endless replacements
which fixed each farm's chequerboards,
with Time measured in gum-tree tops
floating backwards on far horizons.

A Breath of Wind on a Summer Night

A river of blackness curls over
a stone. Just like that old woman said,
talking in her back kitchen at the station
a day's drive from Alice. You hear it
"like a breath of wind when you don't expect it."
I'd met the oldest of the two children:
children of his own, he now ran the place.
The night before, his mother had talked on a bit:
how that early life, the people camped
round the house—it had all gone. The old woman
(it was her husband first took out the lease) was talking
about journeys she had made: she spoke as
if it was all yesterday. Years back, they'd gone north
to Chambers Pillar, with the first two children,
and they'd carved their initials on a rock there.
Never been back. I did the drive two days later,
took a photo after I found the stone—in that wide, red
country of fleeing ancestors, you could
still find it. Not the pillar. The stone she'd scribed.
It needed an afternoon to make their fence.

The mind's like a razor cutting through water.
All of this—lodged, logged—flashed out
(her voice, those chance words, the stones, the creek)
when I looked up this morning at the black snake
flowing on to the verandah, a flickering
half-caught back of the ear. I hadn't seen it.
A second later black water flowed on stones,
veering away in a quick, indifferent slide, then coiling,
pouring from a bush, dazzling like the
humid, glaring weather which had woken it:
a red-bellied black snake, zig-zag of light
now moving only a few feet off by a downpipe.
It swerves to avoid me as I moved back.
It drains into a garden, hiding there for ever.

It appears (like a micro-second), then retreats,
lurking, buried in shadows, blank as wind
round a rock-face, melting into night.
I respect snakes, no longer kill them, fearing
the suddenness with which you meet them—
struggling under a lifted sheet of old, piled up tin,
or like now (out of glare, narrow lines in heat)
travelling up past the house from the creek's reed-beds.
In grass, they're like trains in mountains, seen from high up.
At night, they're fluent darkness, a river bend
flowing on the edge of a path. Put a step wrong,
it could kill you—all snakes are deaf, sounds
don't make them get out of the way. This one waits,
hangs around, pretends it's gone; then like a
javelin, launches out from between two stones,
swiggling towards the back: its quick meanders
are like a necklace, taken off, and thrown down on a chair.
Now it's heading up to the orchard. They say you get a
sixth sense for them when they're around: that
may be right.

                Other times I sit outside
in the cool of summer night's best hours, catching
the frog-sounds and the crickets, listening
to the night's wilderness, out there over the hills
where cloudy wetlands turn to metal grey. Mostly, as everyone does,
I watch the new stars' spaciousness: instant
flashes of thought, green rock-like memories.
A wind-breath, down the verandah, plays
its way through—a slight cool draft turning a corner.
You know what it is. It appears from nowhere.
It lures you. You must beat it off, take a brush to
the bushes, run up and down, drive it away.
It's just a thought. On that drive to Chambers,
the flat-topped hills (like mesas in the westerns)

swam forward on the skyline. Desert oaks danced out
along a water course. I was younger then: it'd interest
me less now. Yet like that woman on her breezeway's steps,
I sit outside enjoying the cool, remembering how she
talked of sleepless nights. How one time, sitting out,
she'd heard a snake—a brown—moving down the concrete,
aware of it like a breath, like a cool wind
on your skin. And she used that phrase—
that plain, deathless phrase—about the way a swirl
of wind tracks through the night, a breath of it
when you least expect it out of no place:
that breath, that presence, when you don't expect it.
It steps round you, then passes without thought.
Inanimate word or solid thing, deaf as rivers are.
If silence has a name, then this is it: an
arrow-headed stream trying to escape—
a whisper, a poison-dart, an ignored rope coil.

Leeches

They like damp grass, overhanging trees,
boggy pathways, areas without run-off:
they camouflage themselves in twigs, leaves, dirt.
They hang like rubber-bands from bushes,
they sniff you by the edge of the creek.
God's creatures, they're bloodsuckers.
In your shoes they swell like maggots:

fat, soft, stubby. You can't snap them.
Pull them and (as in snake-nightmares)
they change shape, they become more,
they become longer. Pliant to be firm,
they're pastry strings. overcooked pasta:
ideal matter, they're basic in design-
projects for multiples, for being sure,

for randomness. They were very 90s.
Independent, survivors of drought,
they multiply in flood conditions:
they live quietly till they whiff flesh.
Then their tubes erect and their mouths
suck, adhere to, kiss, bruise
any skin which seeps blood. From

being arch-backed, negative, expectant,
they become a swarm. You brush one off
to find another. They pop out like stars.
If they could, they'd be permanent,
returning like shape-changing morphs
whose concept is rain-shower or swamp.
Their bite is velcro. I'm sure, in fact, they're

universal force. If old Galen knew
them as health kicks—as we use fibre diet—
it's likely their role as steady clients

(they search for any source passing by)
makes them vital models for transport,
dispersal, cell-growth. When I discover
them on me, I go round the bend:

out in wet bush, they can be everywhere
yet hidden at the same time. Art,
too, exploits a certain rich dividend:
invention's about naming the air,
the vacuum, with realities yet
to be identified. Text-book leeches. Right now, though,
I still see them as false, climbing friends.

Letter from America
to Antigone Kefala

Wind drifts pollen down to orange ground.
A minor headline for the day.
It sounds like an XPT from Canberra,
pulling up on rails without clicks.

It keeps on going, this wind. It has the
eeriness of what could soon be ice. I can't say
whether it's 'from Vermont' or 'Canadian air':
it takes ages to acclimatise that sort

of detail. Even checking the TV weather spot
is more for show than news. Instead
I have a house, some woods, odd glimpses of
loose-limbed fallow deer, springing off

through greenness—and those head-attacking,
spray-resistant stinging flies which, swirling through
twilight, divebomb at your hair:
I don't know if they burrow in or not. A

sunset walk, up here, is like Bellerophon's
horse: world-shattering ideas for poems
slip out of your mind like coins through a
hole in your pocket, while ghost-like you wave off

harrassing flies. Braving them, I take
a dusk walk down paths loamed with pine-
needles, dry maple leaves, hemlock seed-heads
glowering the colour of orange resin

under tree-filtered, gold light. Somewhere, too,
there must be country without traffic-
noise, either faint or close-up. Far off, it drones
non-stop phasal music (like Phillip Glass

tuned down several octaves), making
background for last year's leaf-fall's prancing grey
squirrels. Like that wind: a steady sound,
marking a change of mood never declared

but always about to happen. Most days,
I write a bit. There's a pool, too. Yesterday it was
the same hue as a cloudless, summer blue
sky out west—like one of those days across the ranges

where a single stray cloud, small as a
baby elephant, wanders in from nowhere
as if grazing on earth's vacancy. You
know the shade I mean. I wonder if

such strong blue occurs here—it hasn't yet—
with the intensity of flat country stretching
under it towards a white lip of horizon
unbarred by hills. I'll let you know.

A while back now, I lived in Spain a year.
There, too, a deeper more exuberant
sense of what lies in between two idioms
suddenly seeped through. I was in a bar:

after weeks of trying, out of nowhere I realised
I was fluent in the lingo, firing back
replies without thinking. Meaning was emptiness.
It was thought, yet not thought. It was obvious: there's no

way through other than to be accurate to an in-built
knowledge of how you feel for things, of
how attentiveness turns its regard towards
pale sky, deep spires of trees, or the stop-and-

go of arch-tailed squirrels foraging in weeds. It
comes from nowhere, from a depth always
to one side of words—like a glance, or a
gaze which strays over someone's shoulder

whether to a gradual, red-grained sunset,
clouded with ember-smoke and pinks or (as
in your poems) to that darkness behind dark,
that dark of late light's houses, of varnish,

of white walls and time's hearth. In
Spain, I got that sense of how to live
inside two languages, a wordless, cavern-
ous space between them, a well of

doves and flowering orange trees: and
you can't be ungainly, provincial-minded,
if you draw from that source. Xenophobia—
that late-made, inhospitable word—

comes with all the entrepreneuring (I
think there's such a phrase) of over here
and over there: anthologies of mates and allies,
dressed up as history. Dead work has no idea

how language works—how things sing
between themselves and their names. That
small yellow American finch was doing it
a few minutes ago in the scrummage of

a still white-fruited blackberry patch. (It could
be the 'orchard oriole' I looked up yesterday,
but small yellow bird will serve for now.)
With its flute-like notes, it's no gatekeeper—

even of its momentary grace—nor is it
noisome like Zeus's gad-fly. The same is
true of the beige-coloured dog-fox which
just now, like a terrier, ran across the path.

Letter from America
to Ruark Lewis

The grey dragon fly is the same colour
as the grey-painted wooden balustrade.
And there's a bird with a reedy, oboe-

like three-note song singing in the avenue
of imported German pines whose line-up
is parallel to the wide-cut swathes of newly

mown field outside the terrace window.
The 8ft deep white-molded pool over there's
been drained today. I don't know why.

Field, terrace, feet: these things won't appal
or appeal to a Mexican-American-
born Sydneysider, but to me they're a

re-awakening of an old language, a
childhood language which I can't quite call
mother-tongue or father-tongue: it's

still at a slant from north country
brogue and grammar school 'accent' which
were, I guess, the birthright I surrendered

thirty years ago. Seen close-up, the battleship-
grey dragon-fly is breathing through its
abdomen: it swells and contracts like a

heart-valve. Its mandibles are jet-black, its
eyes two protuberant white dots like
the spots on miniaturised domino-sets

you can take away for long plane-journeys
or misty weekends in the Blue Mountains.
Photographed, it'd make a study

of grey-black on black-grey, ornamental
as a brooch or ceramic design. Painted—
but it's done that already—it'd be realist

in the way most art here would have
to be, with images clear as creekwater,
capturing a modulated, lucid, up-State New

York candour. This house, for instance, right now
is etched with an exact slate-grey among
tall, down-hanging cedars and a

scoop of grey-green shiny water at
the back where a powder of fluffy
dandelion parachutes wanders loosely

across it. You'd hate the 'out there' objectivity
of it—an example of a school influenced by
photography, film, other image-technologies

with all the longings and absences
which natural things compose these days
as we glance at them and they pass us

by. I'd call that school (I relate to it) a kind of
'migrant realism'—migrant, that is, in the sense
of 'as the Soul doth migrate.' Yet once aware

of this 'thing-ness' of things, every viewer would
guess the work's irony, its angular over-pronounced
clarity like a word hangs a second

too long in the air, undercutting what
the speaker says. The fact is you *could*
be realist here: the settledness of highways, tree-

lined towns, broad waterways through mountains,
and the turn of seasons bringing sometimes
ice-storms but mostly rain, snow, and then

these leafy, pine-scented, bug-infested
summers—encourages confidence in a
history that's studied, researched, known. The oddest

things, like the idea 'ice-storm,' for example, float in,
mind-wise, while travelling: it's an enlightened
state, I think. For a few days or so, an attached

detachment is part and parcel of how streetscapes look,
how peak-roofed houses clutter up a railway. At
times, it could be Australia. Nearly. Looking,

though, makes a palimpsest: you take in
eroded copies of another thing—a
king dragonfly across a dam is captured in

this cute grey one, the pine-tree forest is like
a planting round an old weekender or windbreaks
on those ruined upland stations (started by

ex-Indian officers) in the Snowies. A visitor,
of course I know the name for nothing.
Travelling does this to you. It makes you

dreamy yet still attentive. It's been a habit all
my life and started early. In my mid-teens,
my father, bored with his business,

used to take me driving with him on his
rounds across the north of England: he was
drumming up trade for his imported

Spanish wines—Alellas, rich Riojas, and my
still favourite green ones, *vino verde* or
verdelho. In the glove compartment, there

were the poets he'd always liked—Eliot, bitter
Larkin and the Welshmen, Vernon Scannel
and Thomas (R.S.) He took them out at

roadside stops. Back home at night, he jotted screeds
of 'nature poetry.' He called it doing the accounts.
Sincerely, he hoped I'd do more, with more success:

but "study money, not poetry" was his long-lived, bleak
advice. In his 80s now, his steady observation:
"I've given up making sense of things. Work only

for yourself." A palimpsest is what's scraped away:
a scraping which reveals a trace, a 'beneath' that's covered
over with new scrawl. Are memories like that trace?

It could be so, but they are more like waves, a
patterning of dots, invasive, darting, spacious.
Like dominoes, they fit together, fall apart. Like

stories, too, you have to think them out, make them work.
Recurrent as surf-sound heard at night in one
of those beach houses I often rent to go away

and write, they're always the same,
always different. (You too will have lain awake, listening like this,
imagining the long wilderness of dark nights those

bristling white-haired waves are driven from.) But
unlike wave-sound, memories can be switched off:
you get absorbed in something else. My work

remains, though, about nature or, rather, 'what we
mean by it'—what it still can mean. It's the only theme
we have which speaks beyond ourselves. If my

preference is for country things, that's because
I like places with light, weather, space. Not just
because of style. All such choices are

delicate, often made from damage or a wound
we carry, a palimpsest of
pale bruised cicatrice beneath

its crust of blood. A bird. A grey-blue river.
A dragon-fly. I have to work to find that view,
to get a glance of it: I mean, a trace, a breaking wave.

Scenic Mode

She rushes out of the house,
hating Mum. Who hates her.
She's sure of it—and Dad
whom Mum hates is a no-hoper,

a stranger married to an angry
blonde in another town. Weekends
he comes by in his new Camira
to take her out: she despises him

but can't say what she means.
"What have you been reading?"
he asks. "How's school?" And:
"How's Tracy?" the only recent friend

he's ever met. He'd fronted up
one Sunday morning months back
after Tracy stayed over when her parents
were away. But she fell out with

Tracy weeks ago, can't say
anything to him, feels blank scorn:
he looks ridiculous, quizzing her
about books, shoes, clothes. "How much

were they?" He'll pay for them,
fishing out fifty bucks after they've
pulled up in windscreen light outside
the letterbox. It's a late summer

afternoon. Bleached verges are starting
to go back to green grass. The gate up
the driveway to his ex-wife's
tilts on one hinge, never gets fixed;

the drive's eroded tyre-tracks are like
two baked clay valleys. All he
sees are red pebbles, scored
overhangs, newly seeding fireweed.

*

So she's running out of
the house now. Towards the paddock,
up through the unmown
orchard. Up against the slope,

out into the Spring-time air
where slow-growing fruit-
trees are like miniatures of
themselves, reflectors of four month

summer heat which, each year, holds
them back. Furious with what
she can't name, she rushes past
her mother's stunted ghosts—

those hates and plans and
firmnesses about how life is
lived. Being September, a gash
of white—late flowers on a shoulder-

sized Japanese pear's leafless branches—
flashlights itself for the blink of an eye:
the tree itself stock still, youthful,
yet more permanent than stone,

while the teenage girl runs past
half-glancing at its lacework, its
petal-froth. A snow-blaze she'll retain
ten years later. A windscreen light.

The Coolamon
for Kim Mahood

A hollowed-out shape for carrying things,
a cradle or a water-carrier,
a smooth round space when a stone's lifted out—
its original's made of bark or wood.
The sand hollow left when someone sleeps
in a dry creek bed is its negative; but so could be

the shoulder-sized dimple in a tree-trunk—
a bruised hole—where a heavy white branch
has snapped off leaving a dark, scarred indent
with ants fossicking, or grubs lodged in splints
of bark. (The tree keeps alive, though.) There
are days, too, when an ochre, hill-sized boulder carves

a dome shape from the emptiness of empty skylines.
Blue's sculpted against the hillside in relief,
till it turns into a coolamon. The rock
floats forward in a sea of low scrub;
blond spinifex rolls skywards. Maybe
there's a storm out further west blowing up faint cabbage leaves,

draping white javelins overhead. Even
a photo won't get it right, since photos
put things in a place. Out here is somewhere
where the eye trails on beyond that skyline
and where the whole problem's one of frame:
purple rock-hills appear, then vanish, depending how you go

and when you get out, it's the sharp hoof-marks
fanned in caked mud (it once rained there) which fix
your attention. If there's wind, the Toyota
offers shelter for a fire whose smoke
veers off in the only curling, wandering
shape for miles. There's tea. You unpack chairs like it's a picnic,

staring at how first darknesses stretch out
their dried skins. Let loose, the dog chases off
down an invisible track, startling some birds
which, like you, may have been returning
home or just travelling through. There's no more
than making sense of it as a mid-point in a three-day drive,

some dry watercourse, dimpled and scalloped,
whose hollows fill now with amber-reds, deep-
ening blues: a footprint-covered Bondi Beach when
everyone's going home. It seems this hand-made
shape is everywhere you look into,
cradling the day like a womb holds a foetus, like a scoop

of light pressuring the ground. To see it,
it needs an in-born, and yet practised eye
which knows how ancestors inhabit poems:
as if each act of imaging bespeaks
a corridor, a crossing of the ways,
wind-blown in pinpoints of fire, running like quail through shadow.

Fine Rain at Night

Fine, very slow, persistent rain
with its undertalk of shimmerings and insect wings
has already got to me, is already talking its half-heard voices
round the back of the house or here along the verandah.

It's drifting in arrow-heads through the side-door light.
Now it's playing its late modern ensemble of pings and drum-beats.
It should be recorded, treated, made into a model
of world music—a long-sought harmony between things and minds.

It's played by no-one, designed nowhere, part of the great limit
on sciences, global structure, maths: it defies motive,
it has function. It suggests how most events are random.
Being mere rain it keeps battering on gutters, down drain-pipes.

Being invisible it saunters out of the darkness like an animal,
padding up before you've seen it. Bright, noisy—definitely
a body fanning out across the blackness, sliding through branches—
but more like a face whose expression you'd like to read, and know well:

what you notice is Amazon rivers, lakes, shore-lines, swamps.
That's how your mind's flooded with it, adapting to its miniatures,
which free-fall on verandah-post, wooden steps. It crowds night-space.
Not yet mapped, the gaps in it are like a clear night's stars.

A Month in the Country

Sharp squawks of two rosellas come in with me.
Away from the heat, the outside looks pale and aqueous.
Inside the house, spaces are functional, lived-in:
split-level living, white formica of a dream kitchen,
rimmed round by a verandah giving three feet of shade.
Beyond it, a line of whitewashed, battering light.
becomes a ladder of ripples up the water tank.
The sink's a glittering plain even the ants avoid.
Waiting to grow, the protection for this side,
is a flag-stand of sapling gum trees, still as a crate.

It started differently. Dawnlight: a flamingo slab
where Assyrian glyphs floated on tree-silhouettes—
a sense of see-through puppet-show, with clouds on sticks.
Turning over, I woke to caterpillar tracks,
far flung in high cool, stalking intemperate blue.
Now, away from the outside's drench of light and noise,
the house's anchored stillness is like a river boat's
till the fridge rattles, switching off its cool and heat—
it's unbalanced, it needs fixing. It's a tad too warm
to think of it today. All day, this heat was coming.

An off-the-shelf design, the house rides out my mood:
I'm caretaking for friends, gone overseas.
Their orchard's already planted near a dried up gully—
there's a conservationist half-flush in each loo—
and everywhere signs that they're planning long years
of toddlers' bikes parked on the back door's patio.
These are professional dreams of a two-pump town:
Pajero-land with phone, the main taps town-supplied.
But inside, there are smooth plains of polished wood,
a homeliness where the everyday looks tranquil,

uniform, used—the kitsch sliding screen doors,
doubling for Christmas beetles and security,

or the wood-stove harking back to up-country times,
when fire wood wasn't ever green. Hard to make,
easy to undervalue, it's a new Colonial,
built from near-perfect, unreturning richness.
Half-Bush, half-City, it floats between passion and loss.
No, it'll never deliver the country dream.
Yes, true love's debris clutters the ear-marked family room.
There are fresh scars of bull-dozed earth. There's no pool yet.

So I go inside. Finding their tree, rosellas shriek,
like a detail or a thought I can't get back to:
a hairline crack, an edge of trees, a cloud-wisp's smudge.
Heavy brilliance, overhead, perfects its image
in a few seconds of stillness. Out of nowhere,
a late change might happen, building its haze.
It's not so strange, then, that what catches up with me
is also out of the blue, an electric atmosphere
which builds and builds, unseen like the click of a shutter,
or a blurred thought, steadily brought into mind—

how I've been travelling away from my mother,
highways melting to the smoothness of water,
daybreaks white as saltpans, white as air,
features which, as you drive there, only disappear.
Her death, years gone, is like an outcrop speeding away.
It's seen so differently each time I look.
Long past grief, I hold to grief's inner history,
sudden pain blossoming from something already finished—
a flower-strewn corpse, a memory, calcified.
That's what it is. A grief-sense, beneath things, flashes back,

in a memory of years of illness, themselves like death,
with all your senses frozen, mirror-like, in glass.
I've watched others build anew after the process,
out of families (like my own) classic as *Sons and Lovers*.

Trauma squeezes the heart tight. Time's blank sky
tears down the walls. Nothing is left after the fire.
Like bone cancer, grief fills the brain with razor-light.
It wipes out each start-up frill of cloud-shaped loaves,
each blue-green wing-flutter, each thought of uncupped leaves,
till caught in dying light, maternal, all fear stops.

Forest Kingfisher

The fact that it made no noise
became what it said
including its moth-soft, blue cloak
floating up from a sawn-off stump,

just now perched there on an empty road,
hunched over with his back to us
as if staring at the sliver of orange-peel
poking across the ridge's see-through tree-tops.

Its startled lift was as easy and sure as someone hoisting up
an empty cardboard box, surprised to find it light.
Unwitnessed silence was a falling amber leaf
there in that lonely turning of the road. Then, two things

occurred. First, it breathed itself into a bloodwood sapling
whose inner sprays were night enough to shelter it,
while outer leaves, quivering in late sun's butter-yellow storms,
matched pink surfaces against its splay of azure wings—

it lodged itself under a wedge of sideways glare,
in the aqueous light that pierced the dusty turpentines.
Next, fearing we'd found it, it launched across the space
like someone flying a kite against shattered sun and wind:

it shot itself out of that sapling's nowhere-camouflage
escaping from last light's shell-burst like a fighter-pilot,
a blue javeline freezing the clearing's glassier patches,
heading onwards to where unnoticed flood-swamps glimmered

like coins beneath the trees. It swerved diagonally
across those wells. It was an eye, a glance. It
unleashed its way of being-now, its ghostlike richness,
its stillness flying behind all language that's trained or pure:

blue-jacketed kingfisher, it made off like a scratch on a lens
into an uncovering between eye and mind—*bugeen, muleemah*—
as if it had found a hidden, remembered pathway
down a riverbend's once clear light and the trees' sunset-fire.

The Witnesses

At first I think that they are someone else,
the blond woman and her fair-haired daughter—
it's the car probably, a station wagon
pulling up on the grass, white like the teacher's,
and the profile's the same. But, no, they've found me,
driving in despite the gate's nearly lack of sign
and washed-out entrance turn, and twenty yards
of scratching, noisy wattles. Pretty soon
I know what's afoot or what's likely to be,
greeting them on the edge of the verandah—
surprised to see them, but guessing everything
as I watch them walking up towards me
with the pamphlets. "It's a beaut day," she says.
"Yes," I say, " how're you going." "We haven't
been out this way a while," she says, "but we're here
to talk about God's message." Just like that:
and me, I'm thinking how not to ask them in,
and of how many times this has occurred,
and how many seconds to close the door.
They stand there in the flooded morning light—
the woman with her opening lines, the daughter
glancing nervously at her, embarrassed
perhaps by the whole event—and me absorbed
not in what they say but in the fact they're there.
I let her talk on after I buy *The Tower*.
She talks of her earlier life, what's she's found,
how she now trusts only in what she's found,
how she'll spread the word while the vehicle lasts—
there'll be money to fix it when she needs it.
She talks of a convention down in Sydney.
All the while I watch her daughter looking on,
making the link which holds me, as I wonder
what's gone wrong, and how many phases
this sixteen-year old's been put through to date:
I can't help but think of small town poverty,

a broken marriage and—guesswork this—
ex-commune life, aging, a late start. A
past's dark stream flows in her new-shared faith.
The daughter waits as if the day is long.
Behind her, I'm watching the half-full dam,
a silver coin shining at birdless sky—
it's so blue and bright, the first day like this
now that the heat's over and there's cold.
Listening, I find the woman's motives too frail to break—
I scuff a plank and mention how the neighbours,
unemployed, stay at home, happy at how
talking outdoors has usually got some purpose.
There's no clear way to tell the truth, or lie.
No way, too, to shut out clean winter light.

Sydney Lawyer with Horses

Impossible to focus,
the grass soaking from rain
and the horses feeding on it
with a neck-bending, tearing movement:
they lean forward, then snort at damp cool,
swaying off, fetlock-deep, through green seed-heads
making pale childhood paths up toward the fence.—

They stand there in last year's beaten down grass.
Tired, just arrived, I've walked up to see them.
The grass is still yellowed round mats of gangly thistles
where end-of-drought plantains shoot reedlike flowers:
brown, orbiting meteors with coronas of gold-flecked stamens.
They're swarmed by soggy darkness, mosquito-travelled,
building into ground-mist, itself becoming dense shadow.

It's the place where old rain-fronts stay tangled in rumours.
My own darkness is lost time, a time from the past—
I've needed all of it to see a single thing,
leaving it too late to get going with the visible.
Too late to write a novel, be famous . . . That's the mind-dark,
fearful in this wet grass, speaking back to me. Week-long routine,
lists of calls to make, accounts, things to sign, all lurk here:

they surge back as soon as I touch on such greenness.
*What have I done with my life? Is this enough,
this pastness, this richness from the past? Is this what
years of work add up to? Could I have done it differently,
or better, or with less damage?* They multiply now,
banal doubts, dull anxiety brought on by non-stop age:
a latening greenness, back of the mind, like a valley.

The horses, the long weekends, the paddocks are hobbies.
Even the heavy cloud's red scar is more like an investment—
you see it, take it in, trade it for a thought. I'd

prefer nothing to be blurred, as this instant's quietness is.
Focussed on, some metres off a gutter pings into the tank.
It's a noise could break the self apart. It drops through
all space, all time as if by falling it ripens like a wine-cellar,

its contents stored for years, second by second sinking to a clearness
in taste, to rich lightness, to long metaphors:
the rain's last prickles, for instance, dying into air's moisture
or, like speedboat-wakes, those tracks through the tall, bent grass
or, upwards, layers of shadow hardening under planks of light—
and the way side-lit cloud-flowers (Tiepolo-style, seraphic)
bulge from grey sky. As if I owned them, having seen them years back.

The Red Gum

A camera could catch it. Or a video. A painter can't.
October's first dry wind sifts in across the Harbour.
Rousing, irritable wind, with the feel of flat country out west,
it thrashes the red gum with its tentacle flowers, it blood-red new leaves,
whose images will never be finished, never held, even
by the best of visualists. The reds of this red tree
dazzle and blur, both cochineal and stain of flying-ants.

So I'm stuck with a red tree. With blue waters. Everything's primary.
Gusts and gusts of invisible wind shake the branches
into horse-heads, neighing and rearing, into shoals of silver—
let loose, they're mares floury with dusty evening light
under trees, in a paddock, back of the mind. Spring wind blasts them,
turns them back to main-street bunting rattling, triangular, overhead.
It crackles the leaves like a fire that's burning up too fast, too dry.
Against grey-blue water, the red gum's sinewy branches shine.
Behind it, yacht masts and yellow water taxis cutting their wakes.
Across the bay, particles of cars glide by, silent as a museum's dust.

I make coffee, think of the washing. I'll spend the day looking at pictures:
slides of someone's work. There'll be lunch, maybe a half hour at the
         indoors pool.
All the while, the red tree flickers and threshes, an image from a shaky
         aerial.
Against the blue, its curtain's like a crimson smear, a fishing-net of shadows.
All morning the flat is full of slanting diamond light and sun,
probing, like a philosopher, this side and that. A wall, a bit
of floor, a bookshelf: and, then, again the tree,
like a gigantic window-cleaner, looming at the window. No Oak
of Dodona, its variable upsets the equation. Its clouds glitter,
promising richness, quite other than a tranquil view,
an aspect taken in across the land: a prospect of water-meadows,
a few cows. Or a portrait with brilliant drapery. Who was it
said the wind is "boneless?" The ghost's rattling its maracca,
making words impossible. All the time, this storm-tossed red gum

burns its way into the mind, under thought and reference,
like a premonition you can't tease out:
its own forest of sun-lit fire taking over everything around it,
whether neighbouring roofs or the gulls battling to the Heads,
with rain-storms of flowers hanging out, drily, for heat and bees.
Just for a second, it's static under cloudless light, golden as a haystack.

Stopping For A Walk In Reserved Land Near Murra Murra

It's a stop-over on a Spring day
when, walking through the bush, I see them.
Bees. Wild bees, already clustered,

already swarmed. A galaxy of living honey,
they hang on a branch
in a swollen, brown gourd, a primitive shape

caught on the move. All gouache, clay, and bubble,
it's hard to fix it for what it is,
frightening to imagine stumbling into its pelting dust,

having just landed from the horizon's blue planes
of Spring light, dwarf ti-tree, red earth.
Pummeled soil, hanging between sky and ground,

it takes on a flickering gold-dyed sheen,
gold as in a strand of hair
that's threaded, quartz-like, in that ochre mass: bodies, heads, legs,

writhing on each other, pinioned there.
It's as if each is already a future cell.
Or as if the air has opened up a hasty, war-time grave

where corpses, tossed into the pit, drown each other
with their awkward, rotting limbs.
This swarm is that exposed. That stark.

A wattle-and-daub affair, compacted
in a furious swerve
to a taller tree's white branch, the swarm hangs there

sandstorm-brown,
a haze of movement
and molecules. It's as sharp and deafening

as if all the body's sensations arrive
at one go, or as if a life-time's
thoughts are suddenly, spontaneously, recalled

by someone moving, at the very edge of life,
when the mind's
sky-white with memories, swelling with

the fruit of experience, swarming
at death,
yet holding all feelings together;

or as if, veil-like, it's summed up later (generations later,
after the earth
has soaked up spilt blood and honey-streams)

by the philosopher who says:
Things are not things,
but groups, sets, swarms, flux—

playing their music of ant
and bird. The swarm
is light. It's energy. Fruit of the desert's edge.

Fruit, indeed, is fruit. Yet, whether
in grief or orgy,
these bodies pile on top of each other:

they're a huge brown pear,
they're an outsize bobbin of unwashed flax,
hanging from a yellow-gum.

It takes forever to focus on. It swirls.
It implodes in the branches,
hanging like a wind-harp

of silk-glitters and half-dried mud
with outriders taking off and returning,
like flies to a carcase. Not beautiful,

dark, full of anger, full of sting,
it changes shape
like a pot spun between invisible hands,

slowly growing bulbous, then tapering to a narrow neck,
in danger of falling apart
or attacking like a Mongol horde

yet still clustering, still forming itself
from Spring's exile
and the struggle of poisoned virgin grubs—

till it steadies its larval magic
into an Earth-Mother drone
of particles, dynamos, ancestral flight.

Remembering Floodwater

Back of the mind, it's the white sliver which is
neither misty trace nor meaningless: it probably
isn't snow, nor that glare effect of a white line
which the sea's horizon can sometimes have
on days when the air's clear as untouched cellophane.
It's a particular white sliver, or smear of white,
like a patch of sand bursting through leaf-cover,
held forever, remembered, from some walk years back.
It's the stripe of light on sandhills towards dusk,
caught just once, recalled, seen again somewhere else.
Or it's untouchable shadow on the white metal of the roof
of the house next door, a shadow that's also a silhouette
of a bougainvillea, cascading red flowers
down the walls, overgrown round the drain pipes—
and, above the roof, three pelicans hanging in the sky
as if they're boats moored in wind-slopped water.

This is the brightness I usually wake up to, or
which wakes me, after a night of dreamless sleep.
I slept like that last night. After weeks away,
I wake up once again in a house tranquil as summer,
a house full of things (lamps, sinks, chairs, doors)
which do not need to sleep. Just for those first
few moments, after I've come into the kitchen,
everything's as calm and cool as the fridge.
Then it hums quietly and the lazy, gliding pelicans
flap their wings. It could be once or always,
like a particular sensation which arrives and goes,
before it's anchored, then felt again. Getting back,
I've that feeling that somehow things
have changed, when really they haven't:
perhaps they should have changed. They haven't.
You're still asleep. The neighbour's roof offers
back a little ultraviolet to the unsmudged blue,
while I'm thinking of the time away, the journeys,

the days and days on arid, high-speed roads. It could be
you're dreaming of it right this moment, curled over
like a slope of land. Nothing changes. Or perhaps it's country light
that's burned itself behind my eyes. Now the trace
becomes that sliver. Like a shadow getting through
the lids, I remember spilt-out glaze on flooded wetlands
with their dead, grey trees still standing there
and ibis cruising down to land. A string of fence posts
wades into the water's middle, before it drowns. Up close,
two swallows, scissoring, vanish across the sun.

The Platypus

A gift to innocence and eye is platypus.
The gift's unusual, including mountainous
flowering wattle under feral elm trees,
amber water varnishing emu-egg stones,
dawn's acanthus-leaf cloud after tramping miles
to spy on rare animals, once unprotected:

flat-footed platypus, Gr. for "walking problem,"
botanist Banks gave it to Napoleon.
Its history's famous. Paradox or thorn
in the side of Victorian scientists,
now it's a cute, duck-billed rarity,
an icon for postage stamps. Imagine it, then,

an animal too finely balanced to be seen.
If you want a lithe, underwater Kieren
Perkins—it's a platypus. If you're keen
on Chinese acrobats, you've yet to see
a platypus chasing droplets like a kitten
playing mock kills with a tangled ball of wool.

Platypus also carries with it streaks
of dawn's cinder-glow on water, ferrying creaks
with its alligator-style head. It's no snake's.
Sultry daybreak, dusk's pink slants, are the times
for its water beetle chase, at one with noiseless
swallows darting over the stream's bakelite shadow:

but, unlike them, it can shift from one medium
to another—from scrabble to dig to swim.
Fur, blood, bones, it lives out a warm theorem:
how cells communicate with mode and shape.
It's pure exuberance of style. No post-modern,
it benefits from natural history. No victim,

it even shows how to adjust thoughts to
that maya, that dream, where illusion's both true
and false: too much attachment and you
are gnawed by anger, striving with an aqueous
world which shape-shifts like a plant stem, angled
in a glass tank. Too little attachment and

the transparent creek shines up front, soundless
as the visual nightmare of images
which form TV-adapted, bionic eyes.
A moon-traveller's eyes. This, too, is platypus,
scumbling up through a fire-flecked, weedy drift,
paddling, swerving like a diver, to the air.

Then, back down. Better than the funerary
swimmer at Paestum, it slides under memory:
it can regain depth. Lost from sight, it must be
tracked with a torch light under mirrored ledges,
where white roots dangle, raw as bull-dozed forest—
there it penetrates its world of water-sky—

darting through silhouettes of wobbling banksias and heath,
swimming on a knife-edge of height and width.
It's pelt-shadow. Air bubbles track its breath.
Ducks have bills, female spiders poison, but the
platypus combines worlds in its metaphor
of doing several things well. So you tramp miles

in the hope of seeing it: wilderness's smoky blues
give it its moment. It's placed as platypus.
In the National Estate it swims and burrows,
dark bat spread-eagled beneath light's dream surface,
as it rummages through its household water,
urged on, back of the mind, at home. Pure, dumb sex.

Tasmania

Cold winters down there but at least things grow.
Out here, I tell him, I've had to irrigate everything.
True, the heat went some weeks back, leaving April's
sloping afternoons, slant, long hues coming back.
We're standing outside in the stone fruit orchard,
half-watching the colour change, the molten
gold and white sculpted to grey and blue. He's
discussing how he'd like a place like this, bigger
with more paddocks: the dream of living simply is
his alone maybe, though his wife seems part of it.
She's from Tasmania where properties are cheap.
They'll be there in June to look about.

                                                       I've heard
it twice before. But each time I see him, there's
another child, so the chance of selling up looks
slimmer each time round. He's now got three.
Still young, his future settles near him like a shadow
to explore and wander in, testing it for depth:
I'm probably a part of that. So, we keep talking on—
the sun turning amber by the second—about his sense of
where the world's gone wrong: commercialism,
too little self-reliance, too little independence
in the way we feel. More schooling, too: an experience
he would like and knows he lacks, as if somehow
a technicolour world's still black and white for him.
He's mid-thirties, so you'd hesitate to say a thing.
Half sensing it, I imagine some stony discontent,
at not being taken seriously, not working things out.
But, then, old advices are like the night's deep wells:
who wants a waste of hankering, of unfocussed need?
Privately we all go back, I thought, to what we feel we are,
no point in saying so out loud . . . The whole range's there.
Like me, as a bird swerved through, he turned to look,
amazed by its shadow flung between speckled twigs.

There was no fixity, no pause, just speed in thought.
It was dusk's last robber fleeing its scattered crime.
Even the two of us talking outside in the sun's glare
(intense light outlining the plums' dry, dark leaves)
couldn't then see what we were left with, nor expect
how time stayed still, or how the crickets' trilling
would keep in mind. There was enough space, enough
suddenness, as if everything might stay in reach.

A Word

A twig isn't a girder
or an electric wire
though it jumps like a live spot
in its small, green neighbourhood

just as the silvereye—butter-
cup chin, mallow shadings
under its wings—lands there
arbitrary as a word:

caught on the edge of vision,
forgotten in a glance
where nothing is anchored
(not even a pinched nerve would be)

its path is invisible
and its speed a thought's timbre,
its mood a creative move
of bird swerving in a bush.

Rainbow Snake
for Peter Jacob

The blue vase keeps winking at me.
Painted blueness does that to the eye.
Its blueness is a wilder sea, obscured
by curves and sheen. Blueness back of the surf,
with a gull hovering on water's moody heave.

Past sunset streaks, the vase gapes into air,
all ear to what might drown in it,
now turning sapphire in the shifting reds
which race across this gathering dark.
Now it gleams with lamp-light like a snake

camouflaged in the glitter of midday heat.
It takes the passing wings of flickering steps.
The vase stands there, shining, on the table.
Parts are like islands in a shadowy wash.
The body's razor-bright in changing dusk.

Sunset behind it deepens with a mallee glow.
Re-fired by skylines, it comes from the earth,
a bulb, taut, marked, sinuous. Each side's
again that snake. It bends time. Until about to soar,
pure thing, burnished as desert, it builds rock-towers.

Close-Ups

1. Waking

I was about to say how I went out to check.
But the straw-coloured, bare hummock of hillside
has taken all my attention, its thin trees, its rock scatter,
a solitary white flowering gum-tree midway up it,
strangely in full flower, unseasonable for Spring—

blossoming right there on the other side of the valley,
creating some contour for this and the next
cloudless, blue, gleaming sky which is burning
the grass brown, compacting bleached out ground,
starving it, starving roots and roos to death.

Water's gone underground again this year.
The wet's a myth, made by dead photographers,
capturing Sydney streets before modernity:
gutters flowed like dirty channels through each lens,
cobbles were fresh-washed coal. Air, back then, was cool,

like autumn in Siberia. Here, we've seen nothing
but heat for months, so that this brusque hill-slope's
the result—a golden thing with upright strokes of
see-through trees, a shape looming through lost green.
(A race of wild fire would scale it like a wave).

This morning it's stared me down. Whatever day's doings,
they waited and then vanished in looking back,
in looking out, sensing how the cracked, dry earth keeps
soaking up the light. How, too, this light is like
a thought full to the edge, pliant, clear, alive.

It's a line across the roof of mind and eye—
bounding how far anyone imagines what stares
them in the face. The dry hill's a blue hump, blond slope.

It has no aspect, no image, but bodies itself upwards
while instantly—like waking—my memory's swept clean.

2. Roadside Near Hillston

Crow on a fence-post in winter light
sets its acute on a mile of fence.
The driver passing on the red dirt road

focusses flatness on that black event—
its neck and dead-still beak, its indecision
whether to stay or not. The crow

is looking round, about to turn,
about to take off, leaping
an invisible ladder up to cirrus blue.

To tangible, wind-scalloped blue. It's not making
heavy weather out of landing here.
It can float up and take us all in—

take us as part of the land's glare—
as easily as wait and watch us
sailing by. Like a small detail at the side

of a Renaissance picture, it proves that even crows
are fruitful. This one flutters up,
settles again a few yards off. The kangaroo-bar, the rear-side

door, the crackling CB radio, slide past:
pebble-light, flashing in the road, bounces on our eyes.
Behind us, a pillar of smoke, a trail of dust.

The Andes

The blue-and-white scumbled cloud-drift
from far away down here is
like the craftwork skilled house-painters

could do between the wars, drifting
egg-shell white into beds of colour,
making inlays on door panels. You still

saw it when I was a child. You
needed oils (I think) to make it work—
leaking tones under each other to

get a scored, whipped, enamel
effect. Acrylics—the 60s with their
endless, abstract whites—wiped it out.

Infinity and mind-space were the rage
back then, not this haze of folds
and scallops where, momentarily,

closeness and distance merge
in movement and loopings
made continuous. It's why,

for a second, a gliding cirrus-
shape and an infant
sense of things link up

through wood and surface—
all held together, bent, blended
in an intersection

between two
random facts: between, say, a stone's crack
and a branch's shadow, or slanting April light

and weekend traffic on the roads,
or the collocation of a lake
beside a fence with a water-pump

rattling at night, lonely as a star.
So, too, the paint.
The marbled doorways

in a bright half-empty house
collide with today's
over-arching bout of blue—

all of them, background hum
from childhood, blindly churring in the mind,
spanning its ocean. It's impossible

to get away from it—the
blending sticks like an obsession,
a deepness which will not exit,

a splinter lodged, discolouring, under
skin: yes, an irritant
come from nowhere, perhaps self-expelling.

And the blueness? Blue is a river, things
flowing beyond visibility,
signalling a conscious life, or any life

where events, like photos, match
the time and epoch which they have,
but where time (think of it) is a flame—

in other words, just singleness,
a moment of convergence preparing
for the dove-pink parallax of final sky;

while, mostly, what you are slips
out of reach in the trivia
of scumbled paint, in criss-crosses

of thought, sensation, memory.
Like a colour-chart. Or like a splinter,
memorable as the sun. Like a paint-sheen,

where one of the two terms
vanishes when the other's glimpsed.
A scumble, a creamy strand,

mesmeric in a child's mind,
does this holding-job
selected out of nowhere's un-

controlled and lapsing period:
it's as if someone suddenly
should ask about the Andes

(myth, history, *cordilleras* and the like)
on glancing at spilled out clouds, or
absently remember that novelist

who, standing at John Keats's grave
and studying the famous epitaph
about a name written not in

scumbled blue-white cirrus
drifting mind-wise *in vacuo*
but in water's blackness ('who writ in water')

commented on how it seemed
to lock him still in anger, speaking
'in bitterness from the grave.'

Tasmanian Tiger
for Nielma Gantner

To spend a year, at work, capturing a detail
of mist in winter she-oaks and a background
of lucid water glittering through turquoise dusk
in a sitting-room quiet as its fire-warm dark,
working out how the detail holds itself in mind,
and what the reasons are it does not fit the repertoire

of how to track a thing in wing-beats over time,
and why the magpie flaps up outside, steadying the mood
in which it is beheld, objectifying itself
by drawing edges which the eye cannot pass
even in whirring flocks of black-white words,
skeins of similes for how things move far off,

is to be wakeful to a prompt given only once
till it's drowned against the cloud-line's light,
till it's fixed as a move between two thoughts
about dim stag-horn shapes of back-lit mauves,
till it distracts you from a wire brush's fans sprayed
closely on the window, midway up the nearest branch:

she-oak needles outside, that is, with the fineness
of a prisoner's diamond scratchmarks over glass,
forest-needles of a dense Norwegian night,
watchful and warning claws which do not flower
but seed from their own bud-like, myriad spurs
out into open, lake-mirroring attitudes

against mother-of-pearl-with-cloud dusk-light,
all banked up, echoing with wattlebirds and rain,
vestigial traces criss-crossing ice-white skies
like fibres, magnified, seen through a lens,
as if they seem to part, then swirl again
into motionless, hazy storms at each bough's end.

In weather like Tasmania's, the detail gives itself back.
It's taken a year to see how it keeps occurring there,
down rainbow-flickering shores of she-oak trees,
as something repetitive, caught again and again,
so drained of colour in sunset's orange-blossom glare
that, really to see it, you'd change a whole life's path:

ungraspable fineness of dark she-oak needles,
ungraspable, I think, because so fine,
a thing merely visual, meant only in passing
to an observer perplexed by see-through shadowiness,
focussed in a consciousness of time
which freezes now in snowy blurs, then leaps out—

the bush's only tiger, sharp-fanged, springing,
in an image that's sublime, immaculately shot,
setting transparence in oily green-glazed water,
settling blackness in a guarded silhouette,
allowing, at a glance, the past to turn out right:
a museum exhibit, extinct, colourful, symbolic.

A Studio in Prague
for Mirek Jiranek

Plaited bread where
braided strands of dough fold over each other—
toasted, yeasted, aerated with heat—
often woven wreathlike in the form of an eternity-circle
or corded into the shape of a Corn God
or a Celtic Cross (in rural areas
of those countries famous for vampires it's an art
practised for centuries though not yet subsidized); or

the vertigo
of imagining each intersected angle
of body and movement in galaxies
speeding away from each other like bubbles in a cascade of water
pouring through light and time, on an axis
neither up nor down nor flat, so you must—
if you'd grasp night's sheltering raft of darkness—
also invent scarves of energy flung in space; and the

rabbit-warren
of wires, plugs, circuits, dots, thresholds, systems,
matrices, formats, nets, addresses, boxes,
states, cells, storages, memories, most of them burning away
and open to the air, supporting surfaces
glinting like the wastes you drive over in Poland
when its lakes, snow-fringed with wedding-cake ice,
echo with sunset-wind soughing in birch-trees;—can all of them

be reduced to
a glass of milk spilt on a polished table
when you reached over for a crayon? It was a flash-moment,
a flesh-moment. A moment of inspiration. Well, it became
this little disaster. But the trams kept on running in the street,
wilful snow flakes kept hovering outside the window—
down below, people queuing at the stops. All your thought
was of making your picture as soon as possible

while messages
ran east and west, while stars made their nests
over the Steppes' farms, while malleable dough rose and roasted
in its oven. Under your hand, each grass-blade stood out, diamond-like,
on a slope where warm wind reared and tossed—
bob-tailed rabbits could dig there, Mongolian horses graze—
though there wasn't a path anywhere in its huge, green shield.
It was green walked there, wholly visible. It was mind's forest, the eye's:

but I just now
nudged by winter-blue in a half-baked video
remember most your painting's skyline while having a fit of the dumps
about how automation is loss of power when set against
the yearlong limning of expression, voice, hope,
practised in your more ancient style of studio
after wasting a day (you know, an American-style workshop)
watching TV philosophers at work on their highway.

Late Western Thought

There were crested pigeons
whirring up
from the edges of the driveway—

getting lift off with
their high-pitched wing beats,
like springs rattling in an old car.

So you couldn't help but notice them.
You took them in
much the same way the piebald horse had started wandering over:

the horse was a fat-bellied shadow ambling through the stillness
where the light was turning.
Nearby, some thistles: beyond them, the mare and pony grazed on the
        slope.

You'd see none of this clearly till later.
(There would have been your own looking, walking, to account for.)
The pigeons, the horse, the crickets, the dwarf paperbarks were just there,

scarcely visible,
secretly communicative in
every direction like a place where paths, meandering, at last meet.

Sure, a bird had then cried out
as if the moment could go dark with an utter suddenness.
You'd remember that bird as (somewhere) a cuckoo-dove before rain.

(You'd remember it as a whoop, a shout, rather than a call.)
But you would, by then, be walking back down the driveway
oblivious to the clay-coloured light, the pale wisps of grass

and the heaped-up blemish of gravel
which marked some ants-nest, living or abandoned.
Later, you'd say you saw everything. It entered you.

Of course, it remains no more than a story.
About seeing and forgetting, its narrative is the root of compassion,
not least because, afterwards, you must still capture it at one go—

yes, in a single, sharp flame of light—

setting and slanting,
raking deep fire behind the trees (they're black silhouettes on the ridge),
invisibly burning you, invisibly burning itself.

Letter from America

Two white men are arguing about the earth mover:
how to get it down from the truck
parked outside the rail station. It's too humid,
they shouldn't be outside. Stocky, they look like they spend their lives

working with machines—their day-lives, which is to say—working
with the contraptions which underpin
American life, these earthbound flying-
ants, these nooks and crannies of green, rich complexity:

green, rich complexity, though, is an abstract phrase
for something which denies particularity
in this local cybernetic mode of lakes
and highways, dense woods and rusted factories,

invisible and visible wealth careering
down tollways, where labour's become
a non-stop office behaviour, a commuting
between islands of coolness, synthesised voices and a pace

a village blacksmith could deal with, all of it on line.
Interiors are enamelled, clean,
decked with white and gold-trimmed lamps. Future time
is already here, extracted from pockets of memory loss

via thresholds and samples, making it impossible to fall
beneath a level still to be invented
or imagined differently: *green, rich
complexity* occurring if we go forward without things.

Trailer parks will eat up the earth one day, but not here.
Dipped in fire, they'll be tidied away
whether by local ordinance or, as here,
by simply ignoring those lives 'of quiet desperation'—

that 19th Century American's phrase—which were viewed
from a hollow of mirror-like, Ice Age pond
not far from where I'm now: yet those two guys
have worked it out, in green sun-vizors and white T-shirts,

inching the earth-mover down to the carpark's gritty asphalt.
I've the sense nothing touches the ground,
not even this behemoth with its caterpillared
wheels, yellow perspex-glassed cab and proboscis

with half crab-claw, half-shovel prong. Perhaps they mean
to excavate a flyover or an
isthmus with it, thereby adding to the communication
load which their rich, death-seeking neighbours, trapped in time,

are burdened by. On their highways they drive right through that load,
preferring data to be piped to im-
maculate white clapboard village houses
with neo-classical porches where frayed Stars and Stripes

hang listlessly behind trim lawns. Multi-channel television
becomes both umbrella and window,
carelessly glimpsing a diamante storm:
somewhere in there, a necklace of night-time, red-light, unsewered

tropical towns sprawls under purple sunset-pollution haze,
together with the verdigris mudflats of
coastal floating villages and (like an eyebrow)
that pale, elegant half-desert landscape I'm familiar with:

maroons, silvers, browns, splashes of red-flowering gums haunt it,
and haunt me. But these things don't matter
viewed from here. This is the age
of division, of rhizomatic loss, of litter ground down in a unit

with its custom-built, push-button motor. May it never
break down! May it always churn and chur
from that hole in the gleaming sink! May the
Nasdaq keep rising on the basis of chewed up islands

with their jets flying in for cocktail-hour! Their sharp-nosed flight
mimics the ibis landing in a wetland. Parked, waiting for the train,
I'm in automatic stasis, half-caught
in half-thought: a balance between highrise white as a pelican feather
          and a yacht-sail

crumbling in a contrary breeze. Such images begin as tokens—
smears in paintings, memories of photos—
where a moment ripples like wind in tall grass behind a barn
when suddenly light catches it, makes it local, freezes it in corrugated iron.

Summer

The hotel's blue pool has little shipwrecks on it:
last night's mosquitoes, a bug or two, a lollipop stick.
It has coolness, too, greyness and limpidity
together with the slight echo of pre-traffic moments,
shimmering across its transparence, its daybreak light.

Blue tiles, chlorine smell, a filtration hum,
someone's caulked this ad-world image of a dream
for (it says) 'hotel guests only,' then painted it,
cleaned out the pumps, filled it, set it going.
It's a rooftop machine to plunge into, loving its feel.

Exhausted travellers, for instance, sky-dive in its clearness.
Water (they think) cares for them as it lets them through.
Besides, someone jumping in won't worry how much turbulence
whips up corrugated peaks, valleys slopping
into hills, sprayed-out grunge, glistening parabolas.

Stilled, its mirror surface is no more than mirror deep.
A lap-swimmer cuts through it shaping a wake
before he turns, twisting from underwater, like a shark.
Right now, unused, it reflects a city's post-dawn sounds,
unknown bird-whistles and (familiar, this) that hour-long coolness

of slightly lifted pollution which is a breath of heaven
before the heat. Someone's waking up in the building
opposite—a Thai family on a balcony who haven't slept.
They've been outside all night among the knick-knacks there,
a cheaply tacked-up electric bulb in the kitchen

left on:—a washing-line, clamped from the wall
to a bamboo pole on the balcony, sags under a confetti
of shorts and T-shirts. Are they rich or poor
to live in low high-rise in the tourist zone? This might be
wealth if you've moved from an up-country village,

laced through with smelly waterways, green
luxuriant foliage and the spike of a golden shrine
which Americans, heiffer-garlanded with cameras,
walk through. Here, too, there's a wealth of angles:
that family's exposed to any bastard foreigner

who pushes out from the passageway's air-con
onto this humid, half-warm, half-cool platform
where, terraced ten floors above the carpark,
this wind-free, smooth lozenge of water
has been arranged behind concrete tubs in a fake garden-

effect, four square metres of grey-green *pelouse*,
and six white plastic recliners articulating
full stretches of imaginary bodies, sipping
martinis through straws. Those chairs—
the thought's a shock rising over clear, bare seas—

are really signs of death, sculptures signalling 'absence of body';
while quiet water, I suddenly remember, is stagnancy and grief.
(It's water with a texture which seems to look right past you.)
There's always this desire simply to stop. But I drag
one of the chairs over the concrete to make somewhere

to sit, so I can take my runners off. Everyone wears
such sporty clothes, when travelling: Nike, Adidas,
waist-pouches, sweatshirts with Penguins on them
like we're overseas salesmen for a New York gym:
glucose drinks, cholesterol, sparkling mineral water

are the unconscious of its regulation code. More seriously,
I'm thinking what is it lines up a world-famous shot?
So much which, floating, fills up time is already visualised.
What is the accident which drags you to the shore?
What's the moment, focussed not on that family,

but the one which flashes through its web of neurones,
signifying the merest fact of being here, snapped
in this age of debris, smoke and fire? A glittering,
electronic dust dissolves, mind-wise, in a constant
background hum, indicative as a lawn's pink flamingo:

only the dead, their remembered messengers, walk in and out of it,
like figures drifting, ghostlike, on a riverbank.
No Odysseus goes there now with his flasks of blood.
This split second—this jet-lagged moment—fixes my mind on home:
a humane life that's rootless, mindless as summer is.

Night's Paddock

When we meet at night,
this is what I feel:
you are moving under dark trees.
I am those trees, those shapes.
You're the stars moving down the plain.

You're the stars moving behind
the motion of that move,
the inwardness of mood
by which stars and night modify
their space inside a moving mark,

a restless mark, a figure of moons,
of present and absent moons,
of darkness shining on the water-tank,
of dark motion at the edge
of dark matter, holding it, cupping it

as if it's water-glitter in the mind
or a single thread of memory
moving like a herd across the dust:
my own night within me—
miles of fences under the night hovering.

Music

Double Movement

No meaning to this wave's presence or its impact: it rides in and over corrugations and inlets, over gulleys.

Like something which is stretching, like something which is being tightened, it draws the skin away from the bones, it pulls the face away from the teeth. It stiffens a twig no less than it hardens a dead animal's pelt. You touch what is soft and it has the brittleness of porcelain or crude, baked clay. From this point on, what stands out are the scars and runnels, details and small clefts, grazes and abrasures. Microscopic rock falls and dust cascades: this incinerating blanket of shelterless sunlight makes everything easy to dislodge. Convection walls of heat stream upwards from rock surfaces. But then, take your breath on this slope—stopping among its thin scattering of casuarinas and eucalypts—and look around at where, everywhere, it's as if invisible contours have been revealed, almost as if a tide, far from arriving, has gone out and you can now see the timbers of long ago fallen trees, the small reefs which are stone outcrops, areas which make entrances, others which make shelves. A litter of dead, straw coloured grasses is what's left of covering for the ground

*

"Contours gets revealed as if the earth is sagging down over the ground's frame, rocks and fallen logs suddenly visible"

"In the back of the mind, each flicker of wind gets picked up for a hint of rain or fire—studied, turned over, tossed away—given up for being one of those wandering curlicues of air which intense heat brings on"

"They can breathe round you, those small wind-rushes . . . like a straw tickling your ears or your arms"

*

Expectation builds on drifts of high-up cirrus. A single angophora branch hangs out, zig-zagging like a lightning streak. It seems to move

*

So a shore of windless air, invisible as a gigantic measurement is invisible, does nothing—arriving from pre-dawn stillness, turning, arching, building its silver light. What's taken away are the stem-work and light-work of complex, living forms "vague mist turns to nothing, heading east." It's like losing the ability to see a family or a village or the contour of an object; you lose a capacity to see how things hold in themselves an energy or desire. Material and lace-work, material and mud-work, soil so dry that it's cracked into patterns like crocheted linen, wood which white ants munch into dirt: yes, but the deafening quality of this atmosphere is the brutal way in which things are turned into material. Things can be expended, conglomerated, glued together, burnt away. What you see is what you track. The only deep green shade is the flicker of a female king parrot's back and wings against the blonded haze of grass and ground.

Right now, this reductiveness reaches as far as the willingness to risk life. It has so many features outside in the air but it becomes an internal state, a state of mind: a state of disintegration in which you fear to put something out (a tendril, a swelling which is a bud) and risk its death. In the human world too, a dry force is introduced, one which requires everyone to acknowledge a separateness in the relations between living things, in how one person values another. Shadow is evaporated. Shadow no longer reaches as far as the likelihood of one's own survival. What we cease to understand, have never understood, is how places like this have a history of such tentativeness, decade by decade. (The people who were here, who lived here way back, knew this). Momentarily, everything is dismantled, torn apart, dried down to its own dust, locked in a dream of how that parrot's cry, instinctive as a shower of rain, is jetted sideways under the intense sun's blue burn

Fence Posts

The ribbon of black snake (maybe 60 centimetres long) threads itself
round some dry clumps of grass, moving across a rock, its head held
high, jiggling around as if it's in a cartoon. It's young. It's been hatched
only a few days. It's the puppy dog of snakes. I saw it from the kitchen
window this morning and went out to watch as it moved through
the centre of a grevillea and then, surprised by us, it turned back
disappearing up the bank. It goes so fast it looks like the end of a piece
of rope quickly pulled away. It moves faster than someone could run,
panicked, trying to get distant from the house. Not a tree-snake, yet this
little red-bellied black arches over the grevillea's twigs like a miniature
roller-coaster, dipping and climbing. How it did so momentarily took
our breath away. I say "us" because you'd come down to see it, too.
I'd thought (remembering a biblical curse, something about dust and
heels) they mostly had to stick along the ground:

>   the snake
>   like a train in the mountains
>   in the shrub
>
>   why tell it?
>   why call to you
>   about its apparition?
>
>   why speak its

—

A rare kind of pleasure is the pleasure of realising that you've got over
a shock. It's similar to, in some ways more than, the sense of recovery
from serious illness, though that too (like the end of shock) is a feeling
that the horizon broadens like mist clearing from a tree-covered
hillside and of increasing immersion, day after day, in lightness, in easy
movement and pleasure. As if some new bright fluid inhabits the air,
as if sharpness returns in things. I remember looking out once through
a fifth floor hospital window at the darkness of the street's plane-trees

down through a wet winter dusk in Sydney and thinking that I'd never seen anything as darkly sad as that, as gloomy and depressed as the waves of darkness in their branches and the blocked miserableness of the stone wall behind them. I knew, at the same time, that these bleak feelings were also an effect of the slowness of recovery. The very fact I could measure my response to the trees was a sign, in other words, that things were turning for the better. The darkness, the empty wet night, the scatter of golden leaves on the pavement, the unusual "inner city" concentration of plane-trees and high sandstone wall: these all acted as a net in which I caught the effects of my still very shallow energy, the unbearable muscular weakness I felt, the numbing effects of drugs and painkillers. Even so I remember realising half-consciously ("somewhere," so to speak, in a half-worked out way) that for any human being to have died in that state of mind would have required that he or she acknowledge so much unaccounted for unhappiness that the sick person would do anything to keep alive, to move through. To sort out unhappiness. The legacy of sadness (strange, weak, powerful word) is too difficult for others to cope with, for friends and family. I kept having that involuntary thought, again and again. Perhaps it was a realisation, and a fear: how would it feel to think you would never rejoin the daylight

—

Each poem's an event, moment by moment. That's why it's ultimately pointless to compare poetry with music. Poetry has its own event-structure and, despite the poets' arguments, music is a precise language, precise in ways in which vocal language is not. Of course I'm muttering this because it's obvious and there's no point in keeping these old arguments alive. But a poet and a philosophy teacher I had lunch with yesterday after driving into town went on about it together and I didn't say what I wanted to—namely, I don't want all pleasures collapsed into one. I like the way colour, tone, reference can be picked out, chosen again, changed, placed here and there, in a piece of music: with precision and meaning way beyond words. How blackness of trees and snakes lightens into light on water, into light in dark. And no, those words aren't literal. And yes, that doesn't mean that things don't exist or that we anti-literalists don't care for things, for objects, for natural worlds. Have either of them ever played a note? I suppose not. It's part and parcel of the struggle with the shape of a future poem where even transparency's a wall. And it's why, walking back along the dirt road to the house, I was thinking about the transformation of places in memory, how objects are under attack. The mind dissolves and loses them. You can climb right through at any place. More than just tracing the immediacy of sense in a phrase like "the lightness of dust and a storm's passing rain," some deep structure has to come forward in case we lose the object. It could just be a shimmer, a mark. A silver shimmer, for instance, on old wood. Or dry cropped grass, stained with green after rains have come at last. Or the array of boundaries. Their rusted, taut wires. Or the rough-cut humaneness of those fence posts

Breakfast

Anyone up this early—it's just after dawn—is going to be overwhelmed by the glimmering of things. The grasses, the rocks, the bluff and its shelves, inland hakeas, casuarinas, some sort of mountain ash, I'm not sure which. Then the black-veined, opalescent smear of lake which fills up the middle ground, a long expanse of daybreak light on water. Down there, squalls of wind pockmark the water's surface, as if it's been scattered with grit. Up here it's completely windless, while, far away through the air's greyness, the opposite side's wide blond plain starts coming clear—it's a shore of unfenced grazing country (now as I look) dotted with trees.

Dark cover which starts half way up those slopes turns out to be just more trees, thicker, more dense. If this side's anything to go by, mainly storm-battered yellow box and hakeas. Above them, along the ridge's tops a band of white glow takes the northerly skyline. Of course, distance across water can easily fool: those trees are fifteen kilometres away.

. . . Something close to that. (The sky's getting paler and paler.)

Air's already dry, resonant with the months of drought we've been having. Overhead, two streaked vapour trails broaden into hastily brushed scumble—gigantic scribble marks crazily laddered across vacancy. It's as if someone's leant them there, knowing they'd make an optical illusion, puzzling to work out. They can't be Sydney with its curfew. ("Melbourne to Darwin, Melbourne to Singapore," I'm thinking.) And over here: a steep drop down to a fishing-jetty where the camp-sites are wrongly

◊

A crow sheers away in the trees beneath this slope. It knows its *caw-caw*'s been heard a thousand times before. So common I instantly forget it. I'm not trying to fix the two crimson rosellas, either, which have been rough-housing inside a gangly, smashed tree directly to the left. Their presence easily slips beneath awareness, too. They've quietened for a moment into typical chitter-chatter within a high pitched half-squealing. The sound's "sweet": glistening like a stem of blood-red berries.

◊

The entire memory of waking, a quarter of an hour ago, might also be handed back to forgetfulness, incurring no loss. Together with its other pristine sight: the long-limbed grey kangaroo stretched out on the grass with her two young. (It's a while before I see them). The dry white grass where they're lying is beaten down, as if this is a regular sleeping-place. The mother's reclining on her flanks, the joeys are hunched over grazing. When they see me they don't panic but get up slowly. They're eyeing me. Very carefully. Ignoring me, as if they know the speed with which they can vanish into air. Right there, a "vanishing act" is exactly what they do. I look out across a turquoise braid of water for a few seconds. When I look back they've not been fooled. Quiet as noiseless wind, they've left

◊

Too easy to say that could be the day's excitement.

And the results of dawn twilight's scattered happenings?

Why fix them unless there's some pressure, some disturbance?

Isn't it enough just to be a hunter of images, a hunter of things?

Is it the scale of this water which dislocates?

Years after it's been put here, it never quite fits.

Will it never accommodate this double valley's contours?

Are its pearl-blue acreages shore-nibbled, spread-eagled?

◊

Hard, then, not to fit in what's over there on the left, two or three kilometres away. I knew it was there. It shifts the drama of the moment like a sudden cut in a movie. Every motive, every gesture has to be re-examined. It's the rear view of the half-exposed dam wall and, past it, a spur jutting out into the lake: a drowned quarry abstractly chopped out from what's left of a hillside. A sliced half of a hill, cut apart as if by a sea.

So now it looks like an enormous mass of water is bearing down on the rock face: every ripple carries weight, every windrow blusters towards it. The sense it gives (the half-thought-out link) is water piling up before an island's vertical cliffs. The whole movement builds pressure like an immense oceanic space, but then of course there's the wall of the dam, saying: No, this is not an island. We're far over the Dividing Range. This is *inland*, not *island*.

The truth is: the lake's being human, humanly made, offers the viewer a hugeness not that different from transcendence. It dwarfs any thought of it. Only a dream-fragment can be kept in mind. Floods roar down gulleys like a front of wild horses. Natural lakes are (bad rhyme) the sky's eyes. Was I dreaming that? When? (A line close to one already in another poem might be: *This lakes's wind-blackened surface now winks back*. Or: *It is and always was a decision, and could be error*). Yet the effect's deliberate, not causal or dreamlike. It's light on water. It's like a balance, like an equipoise. And then, no, it's not. A rippling lake surface, the water can't conceive that it's here or that I'm looking at it or that it has any connection with desertification, salinity, river silts. For all that, it has to be said that reality doesn't arrive as a lake. It arrives as an angel knocking on the door, pointing out how many things make up a world. Waking up, what it pointed to was this drowned valley, the yellow-box, the ash, the calm night-covered hill, the weight of wind and water. The weight of design and engineering. What it lit up was a complex moment in perception where to conceive a dam's bearing towards human nature requires the same skills as the resolution of any ethically knife-edge, historically many-sided issue. In our time, for example, some Israel, some country in the Middle East. It's exactly at the point when I realise how each drop of water, hanging in these hills, is gathering to fruition that I realise, too, how far the night's behind me and I'm fully awake.

Bronzewings with Lightning

The bronzewings
come through, fossicking
in the pre-storm stillness, pecking
at the car tracks, drilling the dirt
under trees—

choosing such silence—

napes as blue-grey as the sky,
their faces that striped flash
which might happen anytime now,

in the wind-free lull pecking,
then motionless, camouflaged
in the grass,
merging invisibly
in tumbled bark's dry litter, dead leaves,

until they're disturbed
not worried enough to take flight
(an edge of the mind issue),
still walking,
with an irritable glance and
mechanical jutting neck
as if someone's pulling puppet strings
through backbone and breast structure:

they pause, then they make off
into further, deeper
middle distance, a farness
which stretches westerly under trees,
across half-cleared paddocks, wispy slopes
where dry declivities become watercourses,
under hill sides scarred with rocks—

again to rummage nervously, then freezing,
making sure they're not seen
(indistinct, earth coloured rubble),
and when they *are* seen
drawing attention, like children,
to their own mimicking stillness,

such being the quiet which lets them melt
into pale straw, grey stone, fallen timber,
inexpressibly at home in tree-scattered country,
country with no edges
stretched with broken, rusty fences—
a delicate, traipsed through, low grade patch
in need of losing its melancholy,
of being restored, re-thought, re-lived—

the two bronzewings are voyagers here
hurtling through time,
held in mind for a second
under the sky's bowl

both now evaporated into
the grass and leaves

yes, two of them

*

    Things. Marks in the ground. Things tracking bare stony ground. It's what the machine's whirring sound seems like—a bare place with stones, pebbles, small hand-sized rocks. Car noise, plane noise. In fact, planes pass over so far up that they hang inside their own envelope of silence, like white tubes passing across a soundless screen. Sometimes you glimpse the triangular tail-fin, a flash of blue or red.

Striations. Marks in the ground. Pock marks on stone—weather spots, rain crevices. Not the same as the broad marks which late light throws in streaks across dead grass: grooves, stone-rot, revelations of sedimentary lines

Each mark has its own mind, its own reason for being. Each of them lock into invisible structures of word and thought—utterances, humming, stray thoughts, learnt thoughts . . . that thing I meant to say

that thing which could be said

Gaps, in a sense. Though there are no gaps. Closeness, though there is no distance. A full, perfect moment: but some would call it empty.

(two people not aware that they love each other)

(the sky god saturated in blue)

(two people attuned to each other)

(the give and take of love making)

(my body immersed in you)

This thought between things

*

until the thunder comes back, after a five minute rainstorm seemed to have ended the matter. The birds had gone by under the trees half an hour ago, almost as if in another world. A few minutes later, we ran back to the house, even though the clouds, becoming a single thunderhead, never fully darkened the air. The storm fell in diamond strings, fleshed with light, and then in long scattered drops, darting by, in a pattern of flashes and strips. Enough rain to soak the tin, but not much more. It had come through, moved on, as if it was wandering the country, scavenging, looking things out. The air hardly cooled: it stayed thick as a thermal blanket. Later, afternoon started shifting its light, shadows clustering on branches, down the sides of tree trunks

>dull thunder noise:
>it ripples somewhere—
>northwards.

*

Later, too, intense whitening heat would be over for a few hours, a cool interlude lasting through the night, cooling things down, cooling the touch of wood and earth, cooling our bodies, cooling our touch, cooling caves and crevices. Everyone hopes this is what our night is like. Didn't you feel the space then, right then, like the edge of an imaginary darkness? Didn't you wonder at the trailings of steps and voices: across time, yes, but more across your mind. Across you, across the glimpse opening up in you

Did you remember how absorbed we were, lost in the birds as if we could drown in the blended dust and leaves

>bronzewings dancing, fluttering, in the glare

>dust and twigs formed, perfect, like a hearth

>you leaning forward, thoughtful

while, momentarily, the cicadas start up again their wave-banks of sound, like one enormous drawn-out breath, one after the other lapping, overlapping, linking, one with another. And right in the middle of the aquamarine sky-clearing which the rain burst had made, a one-off final reminder: overhead, a last thud, a last clatter tumbling out of empty, clarified blueness as if someone larking around, laughing, inside a timber house knocks a chair over on to the wooden floor with a cracking sound we can hear from outside Yes, like a grenade exploding, a single thunder burst smacks the sky

The Past

The drive back from Melbourne is a patchwork of histories. Back home, after three days on the road, the paddock's new grasses are wind-free, still. At last green. "It's as if it's all making up its mind," someone said to me day or so ago. Yes, I thought to myself, it's true there's a kind of tremor in which this return to green is conducted. Much of Victoria was green, tentatively so. But as we cross the border, the blond dry quality returns: the slopes are straw-coloured, silvery blond. When we turn off to the beginnings of the high country, we skim an unmarked frontier back into green. In the journey's speed, there's both stasis, no-change and, at the same time, there's constant change. In the larger world, there's tentativeness because no-one knows how long these conditions will last. Rainless years, die-back, dry dams, swarms of roos, crop failure, stock reduction, fires, mice plagues—the list is so negative, the particulars so "bush", that you can't help but smile. Can it get worse? It seems—well, how to put it?—that there's a weather *of things*, as well as a weather of prevailing wind, rain and pressure patterns. There's a weather of the mind and of personal senses, a weather of this other psychological "world": namely, a weather of intimate feelings which change and sharpen each person's idea of the world. If it weren't like this, everything would be equally noticeable. Everyone, for instance, would have registered the news of locust swarms far west of here and seen the handful of scattered, windblown outriders flittering across the half-way-between-ankle-and-knee high grass in the back orchard here. But, no, they're here for a few days only. Not many people see them

~

I wake up with a heavy sense of—already the word I want for this feeling has gone back into sleep. Anxiety, a sense of inextricable failure, a heaviness mixed with guilt about something I should have done and could never have succeeded in doing: all of these are part of the name I'm searching for. A single word to name the feeling . . ." What have I done wrong?" is what I am feeling, or, more exactly: "Where have I gone wrong?"

Some deep internalisation's occurred and, momentarily, a rift, a wedge, of embedded emotion stirs up, like a swirl of sand from a fish disturbed in the creekbed, which then filters through the first few hours of the day. I'm a child again, waking up to the electric, tingling sense of negativity—of anger and resentment—which my parents wallowed in for weeks on end with each other: irreconcilable difference, fret-saw of irritability, slur and sneer, moody non-speaking! What a life! Did they ever make up, forgive and forget? A burdensome, bruised cloud pressed into the back of my mind: that's the name for what I've woken with. And the pathetic, doglike sense (only children can be so abject) of somehow having to make it all right, to make up for it . . .

So let's say that the nameless mood is a key element in the breaking down of anxiety. Nobody can be so sure of things, so in control. No-one can expunge, in every regard, the daily sense of living a life divided, of having another life which, always accompanying us, goes into shadow as soon as we turn to look. It's as if we carry in us a forgetfulness the other side of a rift beyond which memory works without connections. We try to recall and immediately we are wordless. We read the character and then we guess——

    (two pears, two small pears, still hard—hanging in their pale-green leaf sprays of old wood)

    (a gash of fruit across the mind)

    (the poet's words about his mother's death: **_those hands, that face, the gesture of a life which isn't any other life but exactly this one_**)

    (the sense that the others, the dead ones, never lose their intimate link with us)

    (how much love is tied to their presence)

    (a chipped stone flake)

~

Along the road winding beside new green paddocks, the already dry dust spurts blowing away quickly, like words just out of reach—"the past will always exceed the everyday"—much as if, in an abandoned house, a phone's still ringing

~

Yet the green keeps on expanding. All the wreckage of dreams, fears, complex constructions floats through it like abandoned machinery, rusted by the sky. Fences and cars go down in it like holiday makers on a beach entering the water, slowly, inching their way, with a hundred different gestures of surprise, a hundred different screeches and laughs. The sound of so many things sinking into time never ceases to fill one's ears: for at a certain point, things only remain visible because they are half-eaten, half-formed, half-vanished (they're all the same process) in time. The simplest impulse reaches from one end of consciousness to the other, from one moment at the remembered beginning to the on-going moment of immersion. I wake up, for instance, with a single feeling of concern and with the parallel sense that the feeling is, itself, a signal—like a sail trajected between water and sky, like a plough skimming between surface and air

About Balance

"peacock-tasted water"

This was a phrase immediately suggested by the delicacy with which the cumbersome birds landed on the tin roof—a step from a branch, the bulk of the body following after it and the tail half-sprayed for a moment—and then by the fastidiousness with which they tilted forward to drink from rainwater—a deep glimmer of it—left in the blocked gutter. (Inside that gutter, I knew how leathery gum leaves were already going black, and how the metal was becoming tissue as it slowly rotted.) Given the intervention of the three birds, the reality was that the glittering water was as purified as, for instance, the convex contour of silver light thrown against a greater darkness in a photo of Jupiter—or like, even now, back here on earth, a spandrel of amber sun, a filmic, silver-orange hue, settling against Brokenback Ridge

I am looking at what I was writing last summer, a year ago nearly. The situation was, I realize, that just a moment before the owners' young black Labrador had wandered over to where the three peacocks were walking round the shed. Cool birds, they started walking away from the dog in a kind of promenade, away down the tin shed's metal wall, until suddenly—as if at a signal, or some other half-conscious decision which can only transpire between dog and bird—all three decided to flap upwards through the camphor laurels, scattering flashes of grey, blue, white and turquoise as they glided (landing with that bulky step) on to the shining roof. Being late afternoon, the first hint of shadow was making objects look more brilliant. The green of the pesky laurels was darker, greener, waxier than ever. The frisky, very black dog was muscular, deeply black . (The blackness was so sleek that the dog's gleaming flanks reminded me of a flashlight flickering across black water in a partly drowned cave——) As the light shifted, fallen twigs, the grooves in the bark of trees, the topside of sinuous branches began to capture thin fliligrees of burning white fire.

Peacocks don't fly. They float upwards, they float down, they float from the bough of an old tree or from the top of a wall: they're very careful to convert their birdlike movement into a form of levitation, as if by throwing a switch they can command free-fall downwards, outwards. Or as the dog and I both notice, upwards and in unison. Of course they make scraping, nail-scratching noises on tin roofs. The memory of seeing their acts of levitation renders such details unnoticeable. Yes, there's an act, a sound, an ungainly stepping forward and outward— these phenomena instantly plunge into a deep well of amnesia, no sooner commenced than forgotten. So that you are left only with a sense of their flashing colour as they move and of the eye-glancingly tentative, proddingly casual tip of their beak-ends piercing the water surface. In the same way, a particle of dust might land on a lens, or a single filament of hair might: where *they're* concerned—no less than the peacocks—a lack of gravity or the choice to assume gravity makes all the difference. Likewise, the movement of our expectations, second by second, in the mind. All too often it seems they slop around in an old bucket. Sometimes, on the other hand, they seem completely extravagant, out of kilter, like keeping exotic creatures—peacocks—in order to manage the inevitable presence of dangerous local ones like snakes. They slop around in the same old bucket and yet, and yet, they spill over in glittering bridal falls, in catastrophic hail storms, in churning rapids, in drifting sleet, in diamond splashes

*

"2002"

People looking back for ideas about the present aren't likely to see the following scene: a man, no longer young, takes the plastic bag of household scraps up to the back of the house every day or so. It's the beginning of winter. Again there's been no rain. The earth where he buries the pairings, cores and old beetroot leaves, is already falling apart under the dryness's pressures, disintegrating into sandy dust. He digs a hole in a vacant plot, an area being prepared for new fruit trees, not far from the main orchard where a few birds are fluttering around. With each spade, sandy earth tumbles back like poppy seeds or mustard seeds: each move starts miniature landslides. Each edge has no edges just screes of falling dirt. As he digs down, a darker colour saturates the earth. It's a colour unlikely to stay for the wind today has been westerly, Spring-like, a clothes dryer. It's brought a sudden last belt of heat. The hole will need netting and stones over it. There are wombats and they dig up anything from the kitchen which aspires to compost. Why should anyone see this scene? remember it?

It's not that the scene is abject. Even if the idiotic word "compost" is. There's no disgust, shame, unreconciled sadness in the action. It's not just that it's dull—though it is. Its everydayness is just every day and, yes, it certainly isn't a party. Adding in the detail to do with watching a flycatcher doing loops from the branch of a nearby bush will both assist and weaken this everydayness *The air riffles through its wings and, momentarily, that sound connects with the sound of a deck of cards being expertly shuffled* Yes, it's a play of the mind which sows the seed of interest, even with a phrase like *plastic bag* or "wombats snuffling their snouts into plastic bags"

No, there's no abjection. Abjection would require this to be some sort of recovery scene, as if the man has just recovered from a bout of psychotic illness or as if, back in the cities, there has been total social and environmental collapse after the piped water system had been laced with cyanide. Bending down to the earth's not some sort of ritual, either. The man bends down, turns the earth, bends down again and so on. The black and white bird, its fan tail bobbing up and down in the air, flies in a figure shaped by instinct, impulse, capacity. No-one sees the shape or the space it makes—just now—for an instant. The movement bends, the flight trajects. The bird's eye jets forward in a fast world, the man's hand grips wood and plastic in a slow world: time passes, time passes over itself like two freeways hanging in the air, criss-crossing each other. What goes on slips under consciousness where it can't be evaporated. (That space is like a dark stream, unmoving, with shapes forming on its shore.) Screes of earth slip down the sides. The bird itself glides like water. A space—a small leap from eye to twig—opens up in a forgotten glance

*

"expectations of water"

Nothing contains my expectations of water: expectations slop around in an old bucket. Am I still carrying this bucket from the well? Well, am I? This heavy bucket of expectations: if I let it drop all the water spills on the ground, flows away nowhere, between the pebbles. I feel like saying "towards the cacti", but that's another desert, more filmic, drier, harder, more Hollywood.

Immerse yourself in the water because it will offer you newness, a reparation of old ways and new ways in a psyche gone pulpy, eaten by ants, nerveless.

Does this mean then: plunge into the bucket! If so, compare this form of expectation with what is normally meant by innocent anticipation—and, as in a cartoon, assume that you can jump into the bucket you are carrying in order to escape the full-stretched, out-leaping, throat-aiming lion of your thoughts

*

"the next scene"

There was a sense of things about to take a turn that day at the tumbledown property half way up the valley on the edge of the tableland. Was it pretence or pleasure or happiness? All the emotions were mixed, mixed up. In both the jump from branch to roof and the memory of grazing the earth's sides in digging, it seemed as if all the old presences had rushed forward like the shape-shifting of moonlight on water. There was no question that somehow I would cross that water, not now. It flowed before me like a barrier to all other expectations. I could walk along the banks, pace up and down in the shadows by the rocks, and perhaps anyway I didn't want to cross.

The peacocks' flight turns the remnant of the previous week's rain into an element more than rain or pools or puddles. The earth slips, like a runnel of wind-whipped dust on a road, down the sides of a hole deeper than the deepest diamond mine. Both are movements, both suggest impetus operates even in the smallest instances. There's no place where language stays still and things freeze and suddenly the movement of mind fits the movement of things: even the still image taken when the camera stops can only be repeated, ad infinitum, into infinity, while we—you and I—already have moved on, have changed our minds, have changed every sense of direction and life-path which we once had, have moved from sunny side to shadow side and back again, have moved house, have changed horse, have changed our clothes at least twice, have entirely new sets of friends, have become different people. While all this is happening the mechanical repeat is looking more and more mechanical. The lion which has been stalking me since I was a child has frozen, despite the dry hot wind of the savannah, behind an unidentifiable bush or rock or baobab tree. It's stuck there. Literally. Stuck there because it is described so.

The sipping of the peacock and the slipping of the earth twine around each other like braid, like two strands making a rope. They become events—in their way, important ones. Momentarily this braiding, this conjoining of two life-worlds, could be the only event of such importance to have ever occurred. How they make an occurrence is astounding, no less so than our new understanding of how channels of dark matter have incessantly mapped available space. At the moment, they are mapping all available senses of the world. They—the channels and the earth/birds—act like two sounds whose harmonies and discords trace each other, not because of symmetry, that is, but out of a random, extremely precise complementarity. One builds information where the other is silent. The other offers redundant repetition where the first sends a message. Through the haze, the momentary appearances and disappearances, a structure begins to be sustained, a structure itself in flight, itself in motion, whether sipping or slipping or moving apart like stars do. What have I thought here? What am I making? I am carrying a bucket. I am making something akin to a piece of music, it's impossible to say. I am glimpsing a world, addressed out there, outwardly, but also still emerging from a mind working at the centre of experience. I am trying to get to exactly that point. How will I describe that point? This point has so to speak its own inner level of connection, its own sudden sympathy. It is as if at this point everyone, whether or not they were thinking about water, could notice the potential for rhyme between the words *balance* and *baptism*, the first a dance-filled energy moving across chasms, the second a splash or drift of clear water which cleanses you for life

The Driver

Someone was taping up the road and waved me on,
saying "It's OK." In the verge, a couple huddled over,
two other cyclists standing near them. (It seemed wrong to look.)
They were the half-victims, burdened with guilt, placed in time.
The next few corners—I knew the road—these were my thoughts:
first, the jacket draped round the huddled woman's shoulders
like a blurred image in a painting, a few brush strokes in tall grass,
then, against everything, the youthful no-surprise of death,

then fate's blankness—how it's meaningless, a sky
with a single crow winging its black dot across it;
then the permanence of someone's going, leaving, dying;
then how, walking away, the dead unmake an invisible space
we've always known—they're the unthought light where we all walk;
then nagging fear that tragedy, out of the blue, one day marks me
with its sad repeats: some story—some half seen thing—lodged there
like a lifetime's mood. (Already, writing this down,

I sound like a character in my own thoughts.) A half hour
before I got there, some kid hurtled into darkness,
flung forwards, down the slope, into the year's first cooler air,
like a diver swallow-tailing beneath a pool's shaky water,
a melted body sliding under, broken in pieces.
Along the road, spilt flotsam of the paramedics:
a wheelbase for a stretcher, blankets, a frame for plasma.
It was a film set, a nightmare picnic gone adrift.

I drove on, entering my own thought's valley—
its filtered shadow stretched out to now. Rather, until an hour ago.
I was thinking, testing the season's change, some rain.
First stray locusts had started flittering through new grass,
lifting off, floating onward a pace or two. One follows me in,
to hang there, inside, on the kitchen door. (The bad joke "Choppers"
came to mind.) Outside, greenness has splashed the slopes,
gathering more strongly in the gulleys, on the flats—

just now, too, a swirl of firetails lassoos the back steps' sunlight,
though my mind's filled with what I saw before the accident:
that guy—teenager, really—helmet in hand, geared up,
standing on the first of the bends where the road narrows blindly
before a one-lane wooden bridge. He was flagging traffic,
his streaked blond hair shaken loose from helmet and leather.
(I'd slowed down already, breaking, stopping for an instant.)
I glanced across. "What's wrong?" I asked. Then: "Someone's been killed."

His words, direct, ignorant, spiral across the space.
This comes back, just now, as I step indoors out of the day.
His standing there beneath the trees has got to me,
the suddenness of things with which no-one could grieve.
That moment, travelling at the speed of light, caught me out:
under a glimpse of widening sky, disordered rivers hold their flow,
the pale-winged locusts float up before they whirl to earth.
I imagine rotor blades, and then pale flowers crashing down.

Winter Solstice

A vague mood, a sadness, a feeling as when recovering from illness,
a kind of "whatever it is which is going on at the time" mode—

a defile bulldozered between trees where the powerlines go through
        on a ridge top,
their suspended wires as out of place as a street's tramwires would be,

while, momentarily, the cut-out shape on the skyline (a trough shape on
        the crest of the hill)
jags with deep, saturated blue, an intense L-shape of it, and then

the opposite shape occurs (the reversed Γ completing the hill-top cut),
visible powerlines threaded down the middle of it, from ridge to ridge;

and yes, I'm thinking who lives out here anyway, who needs these wires
to be put through across somewhere, nowhere, out of town . . .

and this thought instantaneous like a shadow reaching out from black
        depth
under rotting leaf-fall, fallen timber . . . no, it doesn't matter to work it out:

we're in the car (talking, silent) driving at the end of a winter's day
through empty hill country west of Sydney and there's this specificity

of light and time (itself talking and silent) (murmuring and flashing)
bounced off the scoured dirt road, aimed at us in the leaf-shine

and in the chatter of endless white against black, black against white
on silvered fence-posts (rusted wire making dry-point sketch lines)

or turned towards us in the immense approach of a gulley side of bush,
with its runnels of dark green against mid-green and its broad dividers:

there, where a paddock stops beneath it and, again, where the skyline
is plumed with eucalypts which the light makes see-through like ferns.

So yes, we're driving in this momentary enclosure—if that's what it is—
which names a stillness in the air expanding upwards, outwards;

and now glimpses, too, of shadows among untended white filaments
where saplings have shot up along the road, randomly exposed

in a forgotten, unstudied patch of ground along the roadside.
It's as if someone wanted to fix it up after clearing it—or a fire's gone
       through—

and then forgot it, letting it sow itself back to haphazard thin trees
in a barrier of staves like ripples in a white curtain, like a concertina's box;

seen like this, because a flashpoint of daylight has struck right there
—*seeped, watered, fallen* might be just as possible as *struck* or *pierced*—

at the exact time that we too could take it in, glancing as we drive by.
(It's a revelation, this light passing, transient, intensely here then gone.)

Of course, no thought's quite like this: so detailed, so hurriedly well-drawn.
Equally, no thing's simple, jotted down, a crude visual instance of itself.

(Each frond evaporates in the sun's crucible of melting, tidal light.)
(The junction is something stray, wandering out of glass and motion.)

It's how I come back to myself for a split-second in the car, shadows
blinding the windscreen as we drive down tree-tunnels of winter fire:

then a space opens out for a half-kept dairy farm, for sagging sheds
near blackberry patches, for spires of thistles tattering lumpy paddocks.

★

Taken in a glance, the power-lines are there forever on the ridge.
No-one sees them again like this, startled, picked out at dusk:

And the loneliness? that mood? Not true to say it's from the ridges
even if cold vacancy's brews up over them from the sunset's last-minute
    light

like a sensation half-identified, half-made into a word or thought.
Besides, is the feeling made more clear, pausing to think it out?

That cold light flickers. Everything about it has wildness, rawness from
    damp air,
hard to capture like a shift in tone, like a sheen no word has,

leaving you vacant, ecstatic, impatient with time. With its passing, with
    its fall.
We must get back home, that voice says. Or: *just look at that sky!*

Then something occurs beyond imagining, beyond capture:
a juncture standing out for a minute glittering in darkness

as if the moment's a wing-beat (crimson rosellas swerving from a branch)
or wind creaking in a gulley's trees (a ripple knocking anchored boats.)

*

I'd say the fire-break gets bulldozed every year or so—
under a winter sky like earlier today, hard blue immersing the world.

At the back of this thought (we're still driving) something so sudden, so
    random:
a mere sight of saplings grouped round a dry creek's shallow curve.

Phrase after phrase things rise, half-form, fall, turn, restore themselves,
words billowing in overhangs of leaves, words blown from the earth's
    bare dryness,

loneliness at the core of things becoming what we are,
loneliness not like the pebble in the road but the track itself

over-grown with the flash of day-stars, with half-memories, with things
            glittering,
with the moment's provocations, unweeded, random like the Milky Way.

I've no idea why I suddenly think of it . . . some token of return and
            rescue . . .
I'd walked up to the gallery the painter Miró commissioned for his work

in Barcelona and they were showing installations by the American, Calder:
mobiles, sculpture, drawings, there in that day-lit, garden space.

The Berlin wall was down, Europe was filled with headlines from the past,
all the buried questions, all the borders, all the powers being recalled.

I was away for a few months, writing poems in a village in the hills,
caught in silent argument with what, if anything, a poem might be or
            hold together.
But there in the Fundaçio they were showing a remake of a work from '38,

the Calder black mercury fountain made for the Republic's Exposition:
it would have been lost in time—all the energy to maintain, restore, re-
            build, quite lost—
had someone not thought to re-instal it, tracing its flowing vortex back
            through those years of war.

For a second (just now) the spectrum's shadow on the hillside is like liquid
            mercury:
its surface flicker's almost mauve. Near it, misty slopes fill with dust-
            sheened lacquer:

on the ridge a fountain burns up in the craggy, sky-bright defile,
with the sun etching it, turning its light into a flare, a cascading storm.

It's what catches my eye, half catches it, (tricking it, blinding it)
as we're heading home in these last sticks and shadows of light,

all dusk's colours turning and gleaming, linking up, springing out,
while dark coverlets of shadow float among the roadside trees.

Now

It will happen
just like this moment
(this moment is nothing)
reaching forward
holding some old yellow wires

in a back shed somewhere,
reaching uncomfortably
across rusted machinery, stacked old paint,
to hang the powerline on its hook—

the dust and dirt of the shed,
light filtered through cobwebs and grime—
the dry earth floor like some uncovered digging—

and then turning, looking round,
at the open slab of doorway

where
just like you saw it twenty years earlier
the brown snake
pouring out of nowhere
out of some unknown grass
by the door

moves forward
rising

to strike,
strike again,
striking and striking

but this time
it doesn't pause, doesn't desist
striking

(in the emptiness, an impulse
burgeoning over horizons)
ripping you apart
as you reach forward
for the hook, the knocked over yellow power cord,
the mower handle.

*

Right.
It could be this is how it is.
But this is not the poem.
For you must say, too, how this moment
so much like death
is no more than rain smell,
the scent of rain on stone,
or sweet river-water raked
along its mountain gravel—

and how that urge
half longing, half anxiety
occurring anywhere—
any action crossing over
unthinkingly
could do it—

how this is so
because it seems to link up time
making seconds into one material,
one density or pressure
(like waking from the comfort of sleep).
Though now—right now, I mean—it's just
the thought of rain,
a remembered river bank,
the see-through movement

of light-sparked mountain water
trapped in memory,
which provokes a sense

of the gap—
electric, *so* sheer—
of space around the self,
the emptied depth of self

which, in its dumb movement
and awkward grime,
was felt then
as now

Plum Trees

What the plum trees were doing
was loading galaxies of flowers
like night sky's sprawling fire
in the middle of daylight.

Space turned into bloom and fruit.
Soil rose into juice and scent.
Electric, shaken, utterly still,
unpruned wands thirsted for Spring.

Like gluttons, the trees sucked everywhere
from hidden water, seemingly nowhere—
that was the ground inside the dark
as we walked dry earth, dead grass.

Unreasonably, not beyond forgetting,
it's that year's dry light which falls away
as if plum trees flare in unfenced shadow,
momentary as thought, or as a trace of thought.

Paddock at Yengo

When he walks towards them they come up
for the sheaf of long grass
he's holding out. They've been
left alone far too long. What he notices
are flakes of fire—
diamonds of rain drops—
scattering from the grass blades, a
mix of green stalk, clover, unripened
seedheads. So they move up

across the paddock, the smaller horse loping
sideways, the mare crossing over
as if something's filled the space,
wordless, expectant:
the man just waits,
half-focussed on the day's brew
of thunder, rainstorm and lightning an hour ago,
the wreckage of last year's fires.
Today it's all humidity, grass rain
turning the surface deeply green.

This moment's distractedness is
nothing to do with lack or
failed inclination. It's just that the
air's stillness—utter rain-ceased stillness,
pure as an empty white bowl—has led to another dark,
another breath, or seethe, of darkness:
a single dove whooing from the trees stays hidden in it,
a half-registered burst of cicada-noise, like a blanket
down the ridge, billows it up,
curves it into waves.

It's just, too, that the horses
trotting over have
sized him up in a glance which itself

travels, like a shadow, across the air, across the grass,
within its own unmeasured horizon, its own sputter
of diamond light. As if she's someone famous at a party,
the mare looks out over the man's shoulder.
The cicadas, the cuckoo-dove, are interrupted by a butcher bird.
What he sees is how densely the rain front
has anchored the horses,

heavy bodied things, satin-
bright with wetness,
dark bulks grazing this fenced in place
amongst the new-grown feed. (Electric thinness, sharpness,
humid thickness: air builds its surrounds, soon passing them by.)
Presence being masklike (a face in glinting water) the horses
wait for words maybe, or company. Then they
go back to cropping grass, rough manes the colour of a
cloudy moonless night bent forward to the ground
in a space green as a billiard top beside the trees.

Suddenly, Trees

A precipitation—
August's light rain falling invisibly
through the middle of the night—
did I hear it? did I dream it?—
a slash or drift of it
back of the mind, in the middle of sleep,
unheard, unknown,
not even heavy enough to play on the tin
and wake me

There
all the same, in the morning
(yes, the cold silver morning I run towards)
hanging in drops along nude, thin arms
of those wide spreading American locust trees
—in summer, they dance with fan-like leaves
cascading greenness over spiked branches and trunks—
but now they carry water hanging in well-spaced droplets
along bare branches,
shining winter crystals against the brown paddocks,
globules fixed there like squirts of transparent glue

> (a previous owner planted them
> as part of some plan
> for shade-trees and orchards
> never realised—
> a few are left here
> by the side of the house,
> awkward and out of place,
> too strong, too refined to grub out)

I'm just walking down the verandah,
looking back at the paddock, the trees—
those wide American locusts—
already forgetting the rain diamonds'

luminosity
as they catch 8 a.m.'s broken light stretched out
over glowing earth—
suddenly thinking what it would be like
to have seen this just at the point of having died,
to have had this moment of insight,
of thought—
then to have gone away—
glancing each thing in its passage,
as the light, the water, the bare trees
themselves glance out to me

The Dam

Two notes, a currawong—
I think I almost didn't hear them. Cold frogs
churr in sunset's spindly reeds

saving the dam from being too motionless,
too much like low down water-glow.
Their churr's a parabola, landing as cackle and rasp,

dark sounds, light sounds, a skein of them,
a beautifully animal thing
rainbowed in the budding cave of dusk.

For a moment, it's the friendliest sound around.
That same moment, all the immense inland
seems to reach upwards, and west, out of cooling earth—

out across ridge country, cliff-drop, shield,
over rock country and slope.
It's like your whole mind's contoured by a line of hills.

What's exposed is this special business, now going on,
of loping shadows,
and the way an instant search-light—something reflected from a river
          —flickers

among white tree-limbs silhouetted white,
then through alcoves of honeyed depths
which just as quickly go to ground

in an artifice of angle and flat,
stretching, all the same, into
the untouchable heart of things.

What do I mean by that? *a heart?*
some things? It's merely a glimpse of light
hurtled in this unnamed place,

a gap, a shelf. Is it more
than impulse, more than a breath? Are bitterness and sweetness—
intensity of sweetness—nurtured

in these lights and darks? Or perhaps
it's the water's blindness, the blue smoulder of it
and the fact that its true source, too, is here

in the heart—it's these things which are worth
a moment's thought *"sweet" "bitter"*
Yet stillness inhabits you like being touched.

So the very least thing to say is this:
how it's not a good look to end
with what might, like fire, have startled us out of words,

just when wintry inland light
burns each stagnant grass blade to its exactest edge.
This edge is darkness, a flash of chrome,

being itself no more than a dark
where nothing can be hidden,
nothing left unsaid—no quick reminder—

other than how the frogs will be the only sound there is,
down there past night's swamp oaks
where a bit of space opens out toward the paddock.

Index of First Lines

A camera could catch it. Or a video. A painter can't	90
A clear stillness hangs in the cormorant's cry	17
A gift to innocence and eye is platypus	97
A hollowed-out shape for carrying things	78
A precipitation	157
A river of blackness curls over	62
A sea-leaf is laid across the bark	45
A she-oak needle glitters at midday	45
A top branch shakes down	13
A twig isn't a girder	101
A vague mood, a sadness, a feeling as when recovering from illness	146
About the yard, about warm air	43
across the slope, emptiness like a tide sweeps . . .	14
After a day of Greek references, lunch, and Freudian puns	54
All water is dusk, or light blenched. Mauve-grey	28
Anyone up this early . . .	126
As in a photograph by a small-town artist	31
At first I think that they are someone else	86
Back of the mind, it's the white sliver which is	95
Beyond the curtains, outside	16
Cold winters down there but at least things grow	99
Crow on a fence-post in winter light	104
Dear Steve, I imagine you are now . . .	34
Dying, a ragged measure, across a ridge	20
Fine, very slow, persistent rain	80
I move to them, vertical rivers	35
I was about to say how I went out to check	103
Impossible to focus	88
In winter dusk, a mindless sea	19
It leaves in my eyes the image of a	57
It will happen	151
It's a stop-over on a Spring day	92
Its odd system knows something we don't	53
No cool place on the verandah	48
No meaning to this wave's presence	121
On looking up at the elephants	61
Plaited bread where	110

Quick as the shutter noise	37
Saplings run down the slope, like girls. Blue-grey	19
Sharp squawks of two rosellas come in with me	81
She rushes out of the house	76
Some days, some voices	34
Some things are beyond talking	60
Someone was taping up the road and waved me on	144
That half-open amber eye fixed on you	25
The blue vase keeps winking at me	102
The blue-and-white scumbled cloud-drift	105
The bronzewings	130
The drive back from Melbourne . . .	135
The fact that it made no noise	84
The meaning of that movement must be found	22
The dark green, the light green	51
The grey dragon fly is the same colour	71
The hotel's blue pool has little shipwrecks on it	117
The ribbon of black snake . . .	123
The shirtless, young	26
The white table, the white chairs	30
There were crested pigeons	112
There's already a fishing boat . . .	33
They like damp grass, overhanging trees	65
This was a phrase immediately . . .	138
To spend a year, at work, capturing a detail	108
Two days later, I see again	50
Two notes, a currawong	159
Two white men are arguing about the earth mover	114
Up here in the plum-trees' wands	21
What the plum trees were doing	154
When he walks towards them they come up	155
When we meet at night	120
Wind drifts pollen down to orange ground.	67
You, the world, the house	24

www.ingramcontent.com/pod-product-compliance
Lightning Source LLC
Chambersburg PA
CBHW022012160426
43197CB00007B/394